AF291587

JOHN HUGHES

JOHN HUGHES

FILM BY FILM

David Juskow

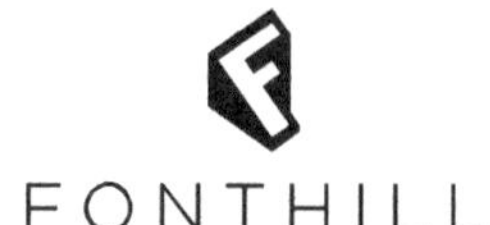

FONTHILL

First published in Great Britain in 2026 by
Fonthill
An imprint of
Pen & Sword Books Ltd
Yorkshire – Philadelphia
www.fonthill.media

ISBN 978-1-03615-200-0

A CIP catalogue record for this book
is available from the British Library.

Typeset in Sabon LT Std 11/14
Printed and bound in the UK by CPI Group (UK) Ltd, Croydon, CR0 4YY

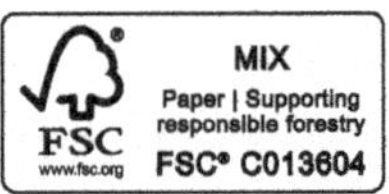

The Publisher's authorised representative in the EU for product
safety is Authorised Rep Compliance Ltd., Ground Floor,
71 Lower Baggot Street, Dublin D02 P593, Ireland.
www.arccompliance.com

For a complete list of Pen & Sword titles please contact

PEN & SWORD BOOKS LIMITED
47 Church Street, Barnsley, South Yorkshire, S70 2AS, England
E-mail: enquiries@pen-and-sword.co.uk
Website: www.pen-and-sword.co.uk

Or

PEN AND SWORD BOOKS
1950 Lawrence Rd, Havertown, PA 19083, USA
E-mail: Uspen-and-sword@casematepublishers.com
Website: www.penandswordbooks.com

Contents

Prologue

Around ten directors have achieved the distinction of having their names transformed into adjectives, with iconic figures like Steven Spielberg, Quentin Tarantino, and Frank Capra leading the way. Their unique styles and dialogue have become so influential that we now describe other filmmakers' work as "Scorsesian", or by directly invoking these directors' names. Despite a relatively brief filmmaking career before his passing in August 2009, John Hughes undoubtedly earned a place among them.

When we revisit classics like *Sixteen Candles* or *Ferris Bueller's Day Off*, we instantly recognize them as "John Hughes films." Hughes carved out a special niche for teenagers growing up in the 1980s—a genre that did not previously exist. Before Hughes's influence, films primarily targeted either adults or children, with teen-oriented movies often resorting to clichés about beaches or malt shops, lacking any genuine narrative depth. These films were like *The Brady Bunch* on TV—enjoyable but far from an authentic portrayal of adolescence.

Hughes made his directorial debut with *Sixteen Candles*, setting it apart from the typical high-school teen comedies of the time. His depiction of imperfect parents and grandparents challenged the idealized family image, capturing the evolving dynamics of the American nuclear family in the 1980s. By addressing this shift, Hughes struck a chord with audiences.

Understanding that creating relevant teen comedies had a limited shelf life for an aging director, Hughes transitioned to more adult-themed films. Although his directing career spanned less than a decade, his prolific writing and producing continued well into the 2000s.

In a cinematic landscape where comedies often receive little recognition from the Oscars or for their directorial prowess, John Hughes stood out. He could have been a transformative force in filmmaking had he lived longer. The 1980s were a unique era for film, and while many movies from that time have faded, a few classics like *Back to the Future*, *The Goonies*, and *The Breakfast Club* remain essential viewing for adolescents.

Many viewers might not even realize when they are watching a film penned by John Hughes, which only underscores his mastery of screenwriting. Known for his rapid writing process, Hughes was reputed to finish an entire script over a weekend. He openly admitted to having little interest in extensive rewriting, confident in his ability to capture the essence of his stories in a single creative burst.

1

Early Life

John Hughes is well-known for his portrayal of the Chicago suburbs in his films, but he was actually born in Lansing, Michigan. This connection might explain why Cameron, a character in *Ferris Bueller's Day Off*, wears a Detroit Red Wings jersey featuring hockey legend Gordie Howe's number. Hughes grew up with three sisters and no brothers, possibly leading to a lack of male companionship during his childhood, and could help explain his later strong connections with male directors and actors, such as John Candy. His father, also named John Hughes, worked as a salesman. In 1963, the family moved to Northbrook, Illinois, a Chicago suburb, where Hughes Sr. took a job selling roofing materials. This transition to a more affluent community compared to their previous blue-collar environment may have influenced the socioeconomic themes seen in Hughes's later film, *Pretty in Pink*.

It was in Northbrook that Hughes spent his formative years, drawing inspiration for the films that would come to define his career. During this period, he developed a love for film and music, particularly The Beatles, who were hugely popular at the time. Hughes also met his future wife, Nancy, in high school. After a brief stint at the University of Arizona, he left college, returned to the Chicago area, and married Nancy in 1970.

Like many legendary comedy writers and directors, including Woody Allen and Mel Brooks, John Hughes found that college life wasn't for him. He was eager to dive into a career in writing and comedy instead. Even in these early stages, Hughes was relentless in his pursuit of success. Back in the Chicago area, he began writing jokes for comedians, mailing them to people like Rodney Dangerfield, who eventually called Hughes to buy some of his jokes for *The Tonight Show*. Despite earning only five to ten dollars per joke from comedians like Henny Youngman, Phyllis Diller, and Joan Rivers, Hughes remained dedicated to his dream, though the modest income wasn't enough to support a family.

At twenty-two, Hughes landed an entry-level job at the Chicago advertising agency Needham, Harper & Steers, which managed accounts for companies like General Mills and Frigidaire. Despite not having a college degree, Hughes impressed the agency with the jokes he had written for famous comedians. Working alongside older colleagues, he gained valuable insights into writing for a young-adult audience. Hughes developed a friendship with Bob Richter, an older colleague with a teenage daughter named Tiffany, to whom he pitched ideas for *Sixteen Candles*. Tiffany's excitement about the project encouraged Hughes to pursue it further.

Two years later, Hughes secured a more prominent position at Leo Burnett & Company, a major global firm based in Chicago. Here, he excelled both in advertising and scriptwriting, contributing to memorable campaigns, including a classic commercial for Edge Shaving Gel where an actor demonstrated the closeness of his shave by scraping a credit card against his smooth cheek.

Another notable campaign Hughes worked on was for Kellogg's Sugar Corn Pops (now simply Corn Pops), where he created the character Big Yella, a pint-sized cartoon cowboy.

After these successful campaigns, Rob Nolan, one of the creative directors, recognized Hughes as a prodigy and assigned him to the prestigious Virginia Slims cigarette account. This role involved frequent trips to New York City to visit the headquarters of Virginia Slims' parent company, Philip Morris.

Although Hughes never felt compelled to relocate from the Chicago area, he was eager to visit New York more frequently. New York City was home to *National Lampoon* magazine, a highly coveted platform for aspiring comedy writers. The magazine thrived on satirically challenging what was considered holy and sacred, aligning perfectly with Hughes' sensibilities—traits that would later define his reign as the king of teen angst movies.

National Lampoon, originally *Harvard Lampoon*, was founded by three Harvard alumni, including Doug Kenny, who later wrote the film *Animal House*. By 1973, the magazine had a monthly circulation of one million copies. It was the premier destination for comedy writing before the advent of *Saturday Night Live*, which famously drew much of its talent from *National Lampoon*'s magazine, stage shows, and radio programs.

Hughes, with his relentless drive and rapid writing skills, quickly became a regular contributor to *National Lampoon*. One of his early stories appeared in the September 1979 issue, entitled "Vacation '58." "Vacation '58" humorously depicted a disastrous family trip ("If Dad hadn't shot Walt Disney in the leg, it would have been our best vacation ever"). Though fictional, it was inspired by Hughes's own cross-country family vacation. The success of "Vacation '58" led to a follow-up story in the December 1980 issue entitled "Christmas '59." Hughes continued to make a name for himself with darkly comedic pieces like "Halloween Rampage" and "The Spy Who Wore Nothing."

At *National Lampoon*, Hughes developed a strong relationship with the editor-in-chief, P. J. O'Rourke. Both were ambitious, and in 1977, O'Rourke envisioned a parody of his hometown Toledo newspaper, which became the *National Lampoon's Sunday Newspaper Parody*. This enthusiastic project included various sections such as National News, Local News, Sports, Entertainment, Real Estate, Gardening, Your Pet, Classified Ads, a color-ad circular, a *Parade*-magazine parody and even eight pages of comics. Priced at $4.95 in 1978, it now sells for around $100 on eBay.

Hughes put together this legendary *Sunday Newspaper* while continuing to work at Leo Burnett & Company. He made a deal with Rob Nolan to keep his *Lampoon* work separate from his ad agency responsibilities. Juggling multiple projects at once was a hallmark of Hughes's approach, a practice that ultimately enabled him to write entire movie scripts in just a single weekend later in his career. Occasionally, Hughes would fly to New York and back in a single day on *Lampoon* business, sometimes leaving a full coffee cup on his desk to give the impression he had just stepped out to use the bathroom—a tactic very much in line with his *Ferris Bueller* persona.

In July 1978, *National Lampoon* co-founder Doug Kenney decided to adapt a popular 1973 parody, *National Lampoon 1964 High School Yearbook*, into a film. This project became the hit comedy *Animal House*. With a production cost of $3 million, *Animal House* grossed $141.6 million, making it the second-highest-grossing film of the year 1978, behind *Grease*. The unexpected success of *Animal House* catapulted *National Lampoon* to a new level of prominence.

By early 1979, everyone at *National Lampoon* was given a chance to pitch a movie, and P. J. O'Rourke advised Hughes to upgrade his "day job" and work at *Lampoon* full-time. Despite this, Hughes was unwilling to relocate to New York, so he continued commuting between New York and Chicago.

Though eager to pitch movies to any studio willing to listen, Hughes was still relatively new at *National Lampoon* and was first tasked to write for the *Animal House* TV spin-off, *Delta House*. The show aired on ABC in 1979 for just thirteen episodes, featuring only four actors from the original film and starring Michelle Pfeiffer in her debut role. Produced by Ivan Reitman, Hughes contributed to four of the thirteen episodes.

After the cancellation of *Delta House* in April 1979, Matty Simmons, owner of Twenty First Century Communications, Inc. (which owned *National Lampoon*) and a producer of *Animal House*, found himself at Universal Studios with Richard Zanuck and David Brown, the executive producers of the 1975 blockbuster *Jaws*. During their conversation, Zanuck and Brown, impressed by the unexpected success of *Animal House*, expressed interest in collaborating on a new project with Simmons and his *National Lampoon* team. In a moment of humor, Simmons jokingly suggested the title *Jaws 3, People 0*, envisioning a parody where Peter Benchley, the author of the original *Jaws* novel, dives into a pool and disappears, only to have a shark fin ominously appear in the water. To his surprise, Zanuck and Brown loved the idea, and suddenly, *Jaws 3* was set to become a *National Lampoon* parody.

Simmons returned to *Lampoon* headquarters and tasked John Hughes and fellow writer Tod Carroll (who would later write *Clean and Sober* starring Michael Keaton) with crafting a raunchy parody of *Jaws*, fully backed by the producers of the original films. The project, still titled *Jaws 3, People 0*, gained momentum, with Bo Derek and Richard Dreyfuss slated to star and *Gremlins* director Joe Dante attached to direct. However, a significant miscommunication arose between the parties: Simmons, Hughes, and Carroll envisioned an R-rated comedy in the vein of *Animal House*, while Zanuck and Brown anticipated a PG-rated, family-friendly wide release.

On August 13, 1979, Hughes and Carroll completed a final 157-page draft, which told the story of a film crew attempting to make a *Jaws* sequel while being hunted by a great white shark. The script included a scene recreating the iconic bonfire beach party and first shark attack, except with Hollywood executives replacing the teenagers:

269 CONTINUED 269

                    MARILYNN
                     (angry)
          Who's driving the goddamned dummy shark?

                   DR. DIRKS
                (on walkie-talkie)
We haven't put it in the water yet. We have a small motor
problem in the pelvic fin.

                    MARILYNN

Shit!

                    SONNY
     It <u>can't</u> be the real shark --Cockatoo killed it.

Sonny and Marilynn know now that it was a real shark. They
look at one another for a moment, then, simultaneously,
look quickly toward the platform.

                    CUT TO

        ----

271 CLOSE-UP-SONNY AND MARILYNN   271

They are horrified and both cup their mouths and begin to shout.

        ----

277 SONNY AND MARILYNN   277

Marilynn has grabbed a bullhorn and is shouting from a
camera position on the bridge of the cabin cruiser, across
to the camera on the platform and to the tug camera.

                    MARILYNN
           (shouting through the bullhorn)
          You! Swim over there! Butch! Get your head
          up. Darlene! Let's see those legs! You --
          get those girls out of the water!

                 (looks at shark)
          This is going to be the ultimate snuff movie!
          Roll cameras! Roll Cameras!

Sonny is dumbfounded by Marilynn's apparent insensitivity.

                    SONNY
                  (confused)
                 Roll cameras?

                  CONTINUED

277 CONTINUED   277

                    MARILYNN
                  (determined)
          We're all going to die, we may as well die
          with a film in the can!

Despite the progress, the project hit a roadblock when Universal's president, Ned Tannen (who would later become a key supporter of Hughes), decided to pull the plug on *Jaws 3, People 0*. According to Simmons, Steven Spielberg, feeling that the parody demeaned both him and his *Jaws* legacy, had reportedly intervened, threatening to leave Universal if the film went forward.

Oddly, Universal went ahead with what they considered the "proper" version of Jaws 3. In fact the movie actually appeared in 3D since there was a sudden resurgence in 3D films in 1983. *The Amityville Horror* and *Friday the 13*th franchises all made their third films in 3D that year.

Despite its commercial success—largely due to the enduring popularity of the *Jaws* brand and the curiosity surrounding the 3D effects—the film is often viewed today as a product of its time, more of a novelty than a serious continuation of the franchise. The 3D effects, once considered cutting-edge, now appear dated and even comical, leading to the film's status as, ironically, a kind of self-parody anyway.

Still determined to replicate the success of *Animal House* in the film industry, Simmons went on to create and produce *National Lampoon's Movie Madness*. Unfortunately, the film was so poorly received that it remained unreleased for two years. In a bid to recover, *National Lampoon* turned to their rising star, John Hughes, for a new project. Hughes delivered *National Lampoon's Class Reunion*, a spoof on high school horror films. Released on October 29, 1982, *Class Reunion* was a commercial failure and a significant disappointment. This flop marked a turning point for *National Lampoon*, from which the company never fully recovered. Hughes, disillusioned by the experience, later disavowed the film, lamenting, "I was shocked when I saw the movie. My screenplay had been completely butchered, and my name will nevertheless be on the credits forever."

2

Vacation, Mr. Mom and *Savage Islands*

With two of their follow-ups to *Animal House* flopping and one being halted by Steven Spielberg, *National Lampoon* and the movie studios turned back to the original *Lampoon* magazine for more promising material, reminiscent of *National Lampoon's 1964 High School Yearbook*, which had inspired *Animal House*. Matty Simmons, who had a deep appreciation for Hughes's work, particularly loved the script for *Jaws 3, People 0*. He also recognized the potential in Hughes's September 1979 short story, "Vacation '58," and successfully sold it to Warner Brothers.

Around this time, in 1982, Hughes was actively trying to sell his scripts and explore the possibility of breaking into directing. Simmons believed "Vacation '58" would make an excellent film, and although Paramount's Jeffrey Katzenberg had passed on the project, Mark Canton, an executive at Warner Brothers, became a strong advocate for bringing it to the big screen.

Hughes was initially unaware that the movie had been optioned, but Matty Simmons soon approached him to adapt his story into a screenplay. In this adaptation, the '58 Plymouth Sport station wagon became the 1979 Ford LTD Country Squire wagon, and Disney World was changed to Walley World to avoid legal issues with the Walt Disney Company. Chevy Chase and Harold Ramis later rewrote Hughes's first draft, shifting the perspective from that of the child to the father. Although Hughes wasn't thrilled about others rewriting his work, he trusted Chase and Ramis more than those who had altered *Class Reunion*.

Despite the rewrites, many elements from Hughes' original story remained intact in the final film, including the father falling asleep at the wheel, picking up an elderly aunt, and visiting country bumpkin cousins. Although Hughes had minimal involvement with the film after completing the script, he was brought back towards the end of filming when director Harold Ramis realized the original ending wasn't working.

The original ending had Chevy Chase's character and his family confronting Roy Walley at his home, demanding to be entertained after their disastrous cross-country journey. However, test screenings revealed that the audience wasn't satisfied with this conclusion. As Harold Ramis explained in the DVD commentary of *Vacation*, "It occurred to me that the audience had now invested 70-75 minutes on the way to Walley World, and they really expected to get there. And here we were, denying them the payoff to the whole trip." To fix this, Ramis asked Hughes to write a new sequence where Clark Griswold hijacks the theme park, leading to the casting of John Candy as the security guard. This marked the first meeting between Hughes and Candy and both were credited with contributing to the film's success.

Vacation became a critical and box office hit, grossing $61 million on a $15 million budget and finishing tenth at the box office in 1983. Despite its success, Hughes expressed frustration in an interview afterward, stating he wanted to start directing his own movies because he was tired of seeing his scripts altered by other directors—a remark that was seen as a slight against Ramis. Ramis later admitted to being jealous of Hughes's ability to understand the rebelliousness of teenagers, something Ramis felt he couldn't fully grasp.

Ironically, *Vacation* was a pivotal film for both Hughes and Ramis. For Ramis, it was his follow-up after directing *Caddyshack*, and he'd needed to prove he wasn't a one-hit wonder. For Hughes, it was his second screenplay after the flop that was *Class Reunion*. The success of *Vacation* spawned a franchise that included several films and even a made-for-TV movie.

Since Hughes's short-lived stint on *Delta House* in 1979, he had begun to attract attention from television producers. Still unaware that *Vacation* would become the smash hit that established him as a screenwriter, he signed a deal in late 1982 with television mogul Aaron Spelling to create a sitcom called *At Ease*—an updated version of the 1950s television hit *Sgt. Bilko*, which had starred comic legend Phil Silvers. *Sgt. Bilko* had been cited as an inspiration by many successful writers of the 80s and 90s, including Larry David. Unfortunately, *At Ease* only lasted fourteen episodes before it was canceled on June 10, 1983—a month before *Vacation* opened in theaters.

In 1968, Berry Gordy, the founder of Motown Records, expanded his empire by forming a film and television arm called Motown Productions. Lauren Shuler, who started as a story editor, later became a producer at Motown Productions. By 1978, however, the company was struggling. Shuler had read one of John Hughes's *National Lampoon* articles and was so impressed that she reached out to him. The two quickly became close friends, sharing a Midwestern connection (Shuler being from Cleveland).

One day, while his wife, Nancy, was away in Arizona, Hughes told Shuler about his experience being left in charge of his boys and how he was fumbling through everyday tasks like cooking, operating a washing machine, and even going to the grocery store. Hughes, who had married right out of high school, had never really had to take care of himself before. He mentioned that he had about eighty pages of a script called *Mr. Mom* tucked away in a drawer and asked Shuler if she would be interested in reading it to see if it might make a good movie. Shuler, eager to produce films on her own, encouraged Hughes to fly out to Los Angeles so they could finish the script together, assuring him it would only take a few weeks.

At the time, John Hughes's sitcom *At Ease* had not yet aired, and he still had a deal with Aaron Spelling and Universal Studios. Hughes decided to bring Spelling on board as a producer for *Mr. Mom*, which was initially intended to be a television movie. However, Spelling grew impatient with Hughes's refusal to relocate to Los Angeles to work more closely on the script. At 59 years old, Spelling didn't fully grasp that the 32-year-old Hughes was a workaholic who was always working, regardless of location. Hughes would fax in pages at three o'clock in the morning, and some people later remarked that he was more available than those physically present in the room.

Because *Mr. Mom* was only intended to be a TV movie, Shuler left town to work on the big-budget film *Ladyhawke*. While she was gone, Spelling, without Shuler's knowledge, fired Hughes and brought in two writers from his TV series *Dynasty* to replace him. Before he was fired, Hughes had been asked to direct the movie, but he turned it down, saying he didn't enjoy being around the people in the movie business and preferred to make movies in Chicago. Ron Howard, who had just had success with *Night Shift* starring Michael Keaton, was also asked to direct *Mr. Mom*, but he declined in favor of directing *Splash* with Tom Hanks. It was at this point that Spelling and Universal decided to turn *Mr. Mom* into a feature film.

Shuler remained a producer on the film, and Hughes was still credited as the writer, though he later expressed regret that his name was left on the film. Shuler was deeply disappointed by Hughes's firing and has said, "It wasn't John's script [anymore], and that broke my heart."

Mr. Mom was initially panned by critics, and Universal was unsure how to promote it for a summer release against action and science-fiction films. They decided to prioritize the Michael Douglas film *The Star Chamber* and rolled out *Mr. Mom* regionally rather than with a national release. Ironically, *The Star Chamber* was a box office failure, while *Mr. Mom* went on to become an explosive hit.

In July of 1983, *National Lampoon's Vacation* and *Mr. Mom* were both released, marking a significant moment in John Hughes's career. *Mr. Mom* grossed $64 million on a modest $5 million budget, surpassing the $61 million earned by *Vacation*. This meant that Hughes was responsible for generating $125 million at the box office in 1983 alone. *Mr. Mom* ended up ranking even higher than *Vacation* at the box office, coming in at number seven and narrowly missing out on the number six spot held by the James Bond film *Octopussy*.

That same year, Hughes was brought in to rewrite a script for a New Zealand-produced adventure film, *Savage Islands*, which Paramount had acquired. The film was an *Indiana Jones* knockoff set in the South Pacific in the late nineteenth century. It was one of only two period pieces Hughes would write. *Savage Islands* starred Tommy Lee Jones, fresh off his success in *Coal Miner's Daughter*, and Michael O'Keefe, who had recently earned an Academy Award nomination for *The Great Santini* after achieving popular appeal with *Caddyshack*. Despite Hughes's involvement, the film struggled to find success, and his writing magic wasn't enough to save it.

Nevertheless, 1983 was a pivotal year for Hughes. With two major box office successes under his belt, he finally had the power to shape his projects his way, setting the stage for his remarkable influence on the films and culture of the 1980s.

3

Sixteen Candles

With two box office hits under his belt, John Hughes was ready to focus on his directorial debut, based on a script he had written called *Detention*. *Detention* was a film which centered on five students from different social groups who are confined to the library of the fictional Shermer High for a single Saturday.

Ned Tanen, president of the newly formed Channel Productions, an offshoot of Universal Pictures, took an interest in Hughes and his project. Tanen had a history of supporting young talent; during his six years as production chief at Universal, he oversaw the success of films like *Animal House*, *American Graffiti* by George Lucas, and *Fast Times at Ridgemont High* by Cameron Crowe and Amy Heckerling—all first-time writer/directors. In turn, it wasn't a stretch for Tanen to back another teenage story like *Detention*.

Hughes credited Tanen with having the vision to see *Detention* (which would eventually become *The Breakfast Club*) as a film, even though most people who read the script saw it as a play. Tanen was also prepared to champion Hughes as a director, which was crucial for Hughes, especially since his previous screenplays hadn't fully realized his original vision.

However, Hughes began to have doubts about making *The Breakfast Club* his directorial debut. He understood the risks involved in following up two major successes with a passion project—if it failed, it could be difficult to recover. Tanen agreed, acknowledging that while *The Breakfast Club* was intelligent and passionate, it might not achieve the commercial success they both hoped for.

Hughes then pitched a different idea to Tanen: a film that would capture the true essence of being sixteen, compressing the intense emotions of that age into a single day. Tanen agreed to take a chance on Hughes's *Detention* project if Hughes first made the film that would become *Sixteen Candles*. Tanen would finance the film as a low-budget production with a $1 million budget.

As Hughes was going through headshots for potential cast members for *The Breakfast Club*, he came across a photo of Molly Ringwald—a pale-skinned, red-haired girl with tired eyes and unconventional beauty. He was immediately struck by her image and pinned her picture to the bulletin board by his desk. Over the Fourth of July weekend in 1983, inspired by Ringwald, Hughes wrote *Sixteen Candles*.

Sixteen Candles was a simple coming-of-age story about a girl whose family forgets her sixteenth birthday due to her older sister's wedding. Although the plot was straightforward, Hughes infused the story with much more depth, and Ringwald became his muse. The two even shared the same birthday, February 18th, though Hughes had yet to meet her.

When it came time to cast *Sixteen Candles*, Hughes requested a meeting with Ringwald and her mother. Ringwald, who was fifteen at the time, had appeared in the first season of the television show *The Facts of Life* and in Paul Mazursky's modern-day film adaptation of *The Tempest* in 1983. Instead of holding a formal audition, Hughes and Ringwald simply talked, and he found her to be a normal, relatable high school girl. Despite his initial instinct that she was perfect for the role of Samantha, Hughes went back and forth between New York and Chicago to read other actresses, including Ally Sheedy, who came very close to landing the role and would later be cast in *The Breakfast Club*. In the end, however, Hughes realized that his gut feeling was right— Molly Ringwald was the one he had clearly written the part for.

For the casting of Anthony Michael Hall as "the geek" or "Farmer Ted" in *Sixteen Candles*, John Hughes had already seen an early cut of *Vacation* and was particularly impressed by a scene in the desert between Chevy Chase and Anthony Michael Hall. In that scene, Hall managed to upstage Chase, the seasoned comedian, an incredible achievement for a 13-year-old actor. Hughes knew Hall had something special.

At one point, Jim Carrey was considered for the role of "The Geek," but when Hall came in to audition, Hughes immediately knew he had found the right actor. Hughes later said, "Every single kid who came in to read for the part did the whole stereotyped high school nerd thing—thick glasses, ballpoint pens in the pocket, white socks. But when Michael came in, he played it straight, like a real human being. I knew right at that moment that I'd found my geek."

As for casting the character of Jake Ryan, Sam's crush, Hughes entrusted that task to casting director Jackie Burch. Burch had met with Viggo Mortensen, who would later become famous for his role in *The Lord of the Rings*, but she felt he was too quiet and didn't quite fit the part. She even mentioned that his accent was noticeable, which might have contributed to his reserved demeanor. Instead, Burch found Michael Schoeffling, a model for Bruce Weber, to be the perfect choice. She described Schoeffling as having a natural sweetness, saying, "He was sad and shy, but there was something about him; he was a real person." This authenticity made Schoeffling the right fit for the role of Jake Ryan.

Principal photography for *Sixteen Candles* began on July 11, 1983, and concluded on September 16, 1983. Initially, the Motion Picture Association of America (MPAA) planned to give the film an R rating due to its content, but Universal Pictures appealed the decision. On February 16, 1984, *Daily Variety* reported that Universal had won the appeal, allowing the film to be released with a PG rating instead.

Sixteen Candles premiered on May 4, 1984, receiving a mix of reviews typical for teen comedies of the early 1980s. However, many critics recognized that John Hughes brought something different to the genre.

Roger Ebert, writing for the *Chicago Sun-Times* on the day of the film's release, praised Hughes, stating, "Writer and director John Hughes doesn't treat them as subjects for exploitation; he listens to these kids." Similarly, Janet Maslin from *The New York Times* noted the film's unique charm, beginning her review with, "John Hughes's *16 Candles* is a cuter and better-natured teen comedy than most."

At the box office, *Sixteen Candles* opened in second place during the week of May 4, 1984, just behind *Breakin'*, the first breakdancing movie ever made. It managed to outperform films like *Romancing the Stone* and *Police Academy*, which had already been in theaters for over a month. By the end of the year, *Sixteen Candles* had grossed $24 million on a $6.5 million budget, ranking thirty-seventh in the 1984 box office. While it wasn't a blockbuster, the film's success—tripling its budget—enabled John Hughes to continue pursuing his larger ambition and allowed him to create his more intimate and personal upcoming film.

On June 5, 2005, *USA Today* reported that Molly Ringwald was rumored to be in the early stages of producing a sequel to *Sixteen Candles*. Later, on August 19, 2021, *Variety* announced that a TV movie sequel titled *Thirty-Two Candles* was in development, although there was no word on whether any of the original cast members would reprise their roles.

4

The Breakfast Club

Sixteen Candles is now considered a John Hughes classic, but at the time of its release, it wasn't the massive hit that Hollywood might have hoped for. However, Hughes and his producer, Ned Tanen, saw it as a stepping stone for a more ambitious project. This project, initially called *Detention* and later *The Lunch Bunch*, would eventually become known as *The Breakfast Club*. Hughes was determined to make a film about teenagers from different social groups who are forced to spend a day together in detention. He believed that this concept, which primarily took place in one room over the course of a few hours, could make for an engaging movie and would win over skeptics.

Hughes felt a close connection to teenagers, partly because he and his wife, Nancy, had married so young. He often found himself relating more to the teenage kids in his neighborhood than to their parents. It was from one of these teenagers, who mentioned morning detention and referred to it as "The Breakfast Club," that Hughes realized *The Lunch Bunch* would now be titled *The Breakfast Club*.

By this time, 16-year-old Molly Ringwald had become Hughes's muse. The two would talk for hours, bonding over their shared love of British pop music, which was gaining popularity through underground radio stations like WLIR in Long Island and KROQ in Los Angeles. During the filming of *The Breakfast Club*, the Hughes family moved to a larger house in the village of Northfield, close to where the movie was being shot. Anthony Michael Hall, who had also become close to Hughes, would often sleep over on the weekends, and Hughes treated him like a son for a time. Hughes even made an uncredited appearance in *The Breakfast Club*, playing Hall's father.

Hughes had already asked Molly Ringwald and Anthony Michael Hall to be part of *The Breakfast Club* at the end of filming *Sixteen Candles*. Hall was the first to agree, and his real-life mother and sister played their roles in the movie when they drop him off at school. Initially, Hughes wanted Ringwald to play the character of Allison, but Ringwald lobbied hard to play Claire instead. Ally Sheedy, who had auditioned for the role of Samantha in *Sixteen Candles*, had left an impression on Hughes when she showed up to that audition with two black eyes from a set-building accident. Her dark, gothic look stuck with Hughes, and he ultimately cast her as Allison.

Emilio Estevez was initially cast as John Bender but was later reassigned to the role of Andrew, as Hughes thought Estevez would be better suited to the character. John Cusack, who had also appeared in *Sixteen Candles*, was originally cast as John Bender, but Hughes eventually replaced him with Judd Nelson because he felt Cusack didn't look intimidating enough. Rick Moranis, an SCTV alum and soon-to-be *Ghostbusters* star, was cast as the janitor Carl, but his portrayal as an over-the-top Russian caricature didn't fit the realistic tone Hughes wanted, so he was replaced.

To prepare for their roles, Hughes had the actors attend his old high school undercover. While this was relatively easy for Ringwald and Hall, who were still in high school, it was more challenging for the other actors, who were in their early to mid-20s. Judd Nelson, who practiced method acting, stayed in character so thoroughly that he frequently found himself sent to the principal's office. He even bought beer for some of the teenagers with his "fake" ID, despite being 24 years old. On set, Nelson's method acting caused tension, particularly with Ringwald, whom he harassed in character. Hughes, who was very protective of Ringwald, considered firing Nelson, but after the cast intervened, he decided to keep him. Ally Sheedy, on the other hand, found the experience of returning to high school unpleasant, as it brought back unhappy memories from her own school days.

The production of *The Breakfast Club* was as unique as its script. The cast rehearsed for three weeks as if it were a play, which helped them build the chemistry necessary to portray the complex dynamics between their characters. Principal photography began on March 28, 1984. Filming took place in an abandoned high school in Des Plaines, Illinois. The school's library, however, was too small for the pivotal scenes, so the production team constructed the iconic library set within the school's gymnasium. Thomas Del Ruth, the film's cinematographer, confirmed that the production "never left the premises," and the entire movie was shot on location. Unusually for the industry, the film was shot in sequence, which helped the actors maintain the continuity of their characters' development throughout the story.

The Breakfast Club shares its setting with several other John Hughes classics, such as *Sixteen Candles*, *Ferris Bueller's Day Off*, and *Weird Science*, all of which are set in the fictional town of Shermer, an imagined suburb of Chicago. This town became part of the so-called "John Hughes Universe."

Hughes allowed the cast to improvise their lines and actions, encouraging them to offer input on how their characters might react in different situations. This collaborative approach was a stark contrast to Hughes's previous experiences, where he often felt stifled by outside interference. The teenage cast appreciated this freedom and felt that Hughes understood them, which made the filming experience enjoyable.

Tom Del Ruth took an unconventional approach to creating atmosphere on set. He deliberately kept the temperature high with the heat from the lights, which he believed would create a "suffocating atmosphere" and a bond between the characters as they shared detention stories. Two additional assistant directors were hired specifically to keep the cast from falling asleep from the heat.

The collaborative atmosphere and unique filming conditions contributed to *The Breakfast Club* becoming a timeless classic that would continue to entice audiences for decades as an authentic portrayal of teenage life.

According to Molly Ringwald and Ally Sheedy, the original script for *The Breakfast Club* included a scene reminiscent of *Porky's*, where the boys sneak off to spy on the high school's synchronized swim team, only to stumble upon a topless PE teacher. Ringwald and Sheedy felt that this scene was out of place for the film, which was aiming to be more than just another teen comedy. They explained to John Hughes that *The Breakfast Club* wasn't intended to be a *National Lampoon*-style movie. Recognizing their point, Hughes decided to cut the scene from the film.

This decision was a smart move, as it allowed *The Breakfast Club* to distinguish itself as a different kind of teen movie—one that focused more on the emotion of its characters rather than relying on the crude humor typical of many other teen films of the era. At the time, convincing studios to release an R-rated teen movie without any nudity was challenging. By removing this scene, Hughes solidified *The Breakfast Club* as a film that broke away from the normal teen sex comedies of the time.

The iconic dance scene in *The Breakfast Club* was initially meant to feature only Molly Ringwald. However, Ringwald expressed discomfort with dancing alone, so John Hughes revised the scene to include the entire cast, creating a memorable group moment.

The cast of *The Breakfast Club* got along well and contributed to a smooth and efficient filming process that wrapped on April 29, 1984, after just thirty-two days—remarkably short for a feature film. During production, John Hughes captured over a million feet of film, an unprecedented amount for a low-budget teen movie, reflecting his meticulous approach to the project.

In 2017, the Criterion Collection released a 4K digital restoration of the film, which included fifty minutes of additional footage as part of the bonus features. The original cut of *The Breakfast Club* was 150-minutes long, but Hughes ultimately trimmed it down to a more standard one hour and thirty-seven minutes for its theatrical release. In a 1997 interview with *Premiere* magazine, Hughes mentioned the existence of this longer version and expressed an interest in releasing it someday, hinting at the possibility of a more extended and in-depth exploration of the characters and their stories.

By 1984, MTV had become a cultural juggernaut, revolutionizing the music industry and influencing pop culture in profound ways. The rise of music videos as a dominant form of media meant that an intense soundtrack and accompanying music video were almost essential for a film's success. Directors and producers recognized that a strong musical component could elevate a movie's appeal, especially to younger audiences who were heavily influenced by MTV.

John Hughes, known for his keen understanding of youth culture, harnessed the power of music in his films. One of the distinctive aspects of Hughes's work was his ability to integrate British alternative rock into his films, introducing this genre to a wider American audience. His passion for music helped create some of the most memorable movie music moments in film history.

For *The Breakfast Club*, Hughes reached out to Keith Forsey, an ex-drummer and co-writer, who had just come off winning an Oscar for the massive hit "Flashdance... What a Feeling." Forsey collaborated with Steve Schiff, a guitarist for the Nina Hagen Band, to create a song inspired by the film. They wrote "Don't You (Forget About Me)" after being moved by a scene in the movie where Bender and Allison acknowledge recognizing each other in school previous to the detention. Bender says, "I've seen you" as he nods and points to Allison. The song's lyrics also echo Brian's question to Claire about whether they will remember each other after the detention ends.

Hughes, a fan of British alternative rock, had his sights set on the relatively unknown (in America) Scottish band Simple Minds to record the song. However, the band and lead singer Jim Kerr were initially reluctant to record a song they hadn't written themselves, despite their manager Bruce Findlay recognizing its potential for success in the U.S. Findlay arranged a private screening of *The Breakfast Club* in London, a rare accommodation from Hughes, but even after seeing the film, the band still declined.

Forsey and Schiff initially considered a few other artists for "Don't You (Forget About Me)." Corey Hart, fresh off the success of his hit "Sunglasses at Night," and Billy Idol, who had solidified his place in the pop-rock scene with "Rebel Yell," were both strong contenders. They also approached Bryan Ferry, the lead singer of Roxy Music, but he too declined.

When the song was offered to Chrissie Hynde of The Pretenders, she loved it but couldn't commit due to her pregnancy. As it turns out, Hynde was married to Jim Kerr, the lead singer of Simple Minds, at the time. Recognizing the song's potential, she urged Kerr to reconsider it for his band. In a 2016 interview, Kerr recalled how Hynde kept encouraging him: "She kept badgering me. 'I like the song,' she said. 'What's the problem?'"

Keith Forsey also reached out to Kerr personally, expressing his admiration for Simple Minds and suggesting they spend a few days together to explore the project. This personal appeal, coupled with Hynde's persistence, eventually convinced Kerr and the band to record the song. The result was the biggest hit of their careers, and "Don't You (Forget About Me)" became an iconic part of *The Breakfast Club's* enduring legacy.

Simple Minds recorded "Don't You (Forget About Me)" in just one afternoon, with frontman\Jim Kerr contributing the now-iconic "Hey, hey, hey" at the start and the "La, la, las" in the middle. These additions were somewhat spontaneous, as the original demo had placeholder lyrics. Guitarist Charlie Burchill's power chords transformed what was initially a sweet song into the anthemic track that became a cultural touchstone.

The success of "Don't You (Forget About Me)" was pivotal not only for Simple Minds, who gained immense fame in the U.S., but also for *The Breakfast Club*, helping elevate the movie to its legendary status.

The song opens the film, setting the tone as the credits roll into a poignant quote from David Bowie, "*… and these children that you spit on as they try to change their worlds are immune to your consultations. They're quite aware of what they're going through….*" The inclusion of this quote was inspired by Ally Sheedy, who had been listening to Bowie's *Hunky Dory* album and suggested using the song "Changes" in the film. John Hughes, unfamiliar with the song, delved into the lyrics and found that they resonated deeply with the film's themes. He chose the Bowie quote to open the film, reflecting the disconnect between the adults and the teens in the story. The shattering glass effect that follows the quote, transitioning to a still shot of the high school, amplifies its impact.

Initially, the script did not include Brian's essay, which frames the movie's narrative. The original essay used more conventional labels like "crazy and bad," "beautiful and spoiled," and "strong and mature." However, Hughes, influenced by the experience of making the film, decided to categorize the characters in a way that reflected how teens might see each other: "an athlete, a basketcase, a princess, and a criminal." Having Brian read this revised essay at the beginning provided the film with structure, and having the characters repeat it in their own voices at the end amplified the film's conclusion.

The Breakfast Club opened on February 15, 1985, during President's Day weekend, grossing $5 million and ranking third at the box office behind Eddie Murphy's *Beverly Hills Cop* and Harrison Ford's *Witness*. It ultimately earned $45 million on a modest $1 million budget, securing its place as a major success and one of the top twenty films of 1985.

The theatrical poster for *The Breakfast Club* has also achieved iconic status over the years. Photographed by the legendary Annie Leibovitz at the end of filming, the poster has become one of the most parodied in movie history. Before 1985, teen film marketing often featured cartoonish imagery and wacky portrayals of high school life, as seen in movies like *Porky's* or *Zapped*, which were often misogynistic and lacked substance. Leibovitz's poster, however, redefined this approach. The image shows the cast sitting on the floor in close proximity, each character's personality shining through their pose and expression.

Their direct gaze into the camera conveys the anger and confusion hidden beneath their stereotypes, effectively encapsulating the film's themes in a single, powerful image.

The Breakfast Club continues to enthrall new generations of viewers, offering a timeless exploration of adolescence. Director John Singleton, known for his groundbreaking teen drama *Boyz n the Hood*, recalled seeing *The Breakfast Club* in 1985 while reviewing it for his high school newspaper. Singleton noted that despite the characters being white, he didn't feel alienated, saying, "They were just teens finding their way into adulthood–like I was." This sentiment underscores the film's universal appeal, transcending race and time, and laying the foundation for a new kind of teen drama driven by mood rather than plot.

The film not only solidified Hughes's legacy but also contributed to the birth of the "Brat Pack" phenomenon. The term "Brat Pack" originated from a *New York Magazine* article written by David Blum on June 10, 1985. Blum coined the term after following Emilio Estevez, Judd Nelson, and Rob Lowe around the Hard Rock Café in Los Angeles. A specific incident involving Estevez trying to use his celebrity to get free tickets to a screening of Matthew Broderick's *Ladyhawke* played a role in the story that led to the moniker. Despite the label's enduring presence in pop culture, many of the actors associated with it, including those from *The Breakfast Club* and *St. Elmo's Fire*, have expressed their disdain for it.

In recognition of its impact, *The Breakfast Club* has been deemed "historically, culturally, or aesthetically significant" and was selected for preservation in the National Film Registry.

Interestingly, there was talk of a potential sequel to *The Breakfast Club*. In 1987, Anthony Michael Hall revealed that John Hughes had shared an idea about revisiting the characters in their twenties or thirties, exploring their lives as they approached middle age. Molly Ringwald mentioned rumors of a sequel script that Hughes might have already written, a plausible notion given his reputation for quickly drafting scripts over a weekend. Emilio Estevez also recalled Hughes discussing a sequel concept involving the characters as college students, once again doing time together for various reasons, but with a twist: they would be the polar opposites of their original selves. While this sequel never materialized, the idea of one speaks to the lasting connection audiences feel with these characters and their stories.

5

Weird Science

The Breakfast Club made Hughes an instantaneous writing and directing legend. However, before *The Breakfast Club* hit theaters, Hughes was apprehensive about its success, fearing that audiences might not take to this very personal experiment as he hoped. This anxiety led him to create a backup project, which became *Weird Science*.

Hughes was a definite workaholic. If he wasn't directing or producing, he was writing. In fact, the script for *Weird Science* was completed in just two days. The movie, which centers around two teenage misfits who use a computer to create their dream woman, was Hughes's way of ensuring he had something to fall back on in case *The Breakfast Club* didn't perform well.

At the time, studios believed that teenagers only wanted films filled with violence and nudity. However, *The Breakfast Club* shattered that misconception, proving that teenagers could be drawn to more thoughtful, character-driven stories. Despite this, Hughes still went ahead with *Weird Science* (or, as he refers to it, a "dumb-ass comedy") after wrapping up *The Breakfast Club*, as a "safety" because it aligned more closely with what studios expected from teen movies.

Filming for *Weird Science* began on September 24, 1984, after Hughes took a brief summer break. There was a rush to complete the film before or shortly after the release of *The Breakfast Club*, just in case the latter didn't perform as expected at the box office.

The timing was also perfect for a film like *Weird Science*. In 1982, *Time Magazine* named the computer as its "Man of the Year," and in

1983, *War Games*, starring Matthew Broderick (who would later work with Hughes in *Ferris Bueller's Day Off*), highlighted the potential for teenagers to cause mischief with computers. Hughes capitalized on this growing fascination with technology in *Weird Science*.

The title *Weird Science* was inspired by a 1950s comic book series of the same name published by EC Comics, the same company behind *Tales from the Crypt*. Producer Joel Silver, who held the film rights to the EC Comics line, suggested the title. Silver would eventually go on to produce the very successful *Tales from the Crypt* HBO Series. One of the *Weird Science* comics featured a story called "Made of the Future!" about a man who travels to the future and purchases a kit to build the perfect wife. To avoid any potential legal issues, Silver proactively purchased the rights to that specific story, even though Hughes was unaware of it when he wrote the screenplay.

Joel Silver, already a successful producer with hits like Eddie Murphy's debut film *48 Hours* and the Richard Pryor/John Candy-led *Brewster's Millions*, was instrumental in the creation of *Weird Science*.

Silver and Hughes actually met at the Universal commissary while having lunch. He and Hughes bonded over a beautiful woman they saw there, which sparked an idea.

Hughes followed Silver up to his office after lunch, as Silver had just received a big delivery package of EC Comics he was going through. It was after Silver took one of the *Weird Science* comics out of a box that Silver recalls Hughes saying, "What if two kids, figure out a way to make that girl that was in the commissary." After *Weird Science* Silver would go on to produce iconic action hits such as *Die Hard*, *Predator* and *The Matrix*.

Hughes wanted Australian actor Vernon Wells, who plays Lord General in *Weird Science*, to reprise a role similar to his character Wez from *Mad Max 2: The Road Warrior*. Wells was initially reluctant. However, after learning that the director of *Sixteen Candles* was involved, he agreed and had no regrets. Silver was so impressed with Wells's performance in *Weird Science* that he cast him as the villain Bennett in Arnold Schwarzenegger's *Commando*.

John Hughes crafted the character of Gary specifically for Anthony Michael Hall, marking their third and final collaboration together after *Sixteen Candles* and *The Breakfast Club*. At the time, Hall was in high demand, even being considered by Stanley Kubrick for the role of Joker in *Full Metal Jacket*. Kubrick, who had seen *Sixteen Candles* three times, reportedly told Hall that he was his favorite actor since seeing

Jack Nicholson in *Easy Rider*. However, negotiations fell through, and Hall ultimately chose to do *Weird Science* instead. Ironically, Hall also turned down a role in *European Vacation*, the sequel to *Vacation*, to work on *Weird Science*.

Set once again in the fictional town of Shermer, Illinois, *Weird Science* was filmed at the same high school used in *Sixteen Candles*, further establishing what would later be known as the "John Hughes Universe."

The role of Lisa, the woman created by Gary (Hall) and Wyatt (Ilan Mitchell-Smith), was highly sought after, with actresses like Demi Moore and Robin Wright auditioning for the part. Initially, model Kelly Emberg was cast as Lisa, but she was replaced after a few days of filming. According to an August 2, 2019 *Hollywood Life* article, Kelly LeBrock initially turned down the role because she said she was working on a movie with Sting in the South of France and wanted to spend more time "hanging out with Sting." In reality, she wasn't making a film with him at all. Her first husband, producer Victor Drai, was behind the 1985 movie *The Bride*, which starred Sting and Jennifer Beals, and LeBrock became infatuated with Sting during the production, following him around the set. Her marriage to Drai ended shortly after the film's release.

Ironically, *The Bride* was based on *Frankenstein*, and Sting's character literally creates a woman in the story. One can't help but wonder whether working in close proximity to a modern retelling of *Frankenstein* played any part in LeBrock's decision to eventually say yes to *Weird Science*.

After they fired Emberg, they asked LeBrock again and she flew immediately to the set. LeBrock remembers that the crew didn't even have time to change the wardrobe from the previous actress' size to hers. She is quoted as saying, "They literally cut the back of the dresses because I had bigger boobies and there was no way I was going to fit in them so they just slit everything up the back."

Hughes named the character Lisa after the Apple Lisa computer, although the computer used in the movie was actually a Memotech MTX512, a brand that went out of business soon after the film's release.

Ilan Mitchell-Smith, who played Wyatt, was relatively unknown at the time, having only appeared in *The Wild Life*, a less successful follow-up to *Fast Times at Ridgemont High* written by Cameron Crowe. *The Wild Life* was not a very popular or successful movie but must have been a favorite of Hughes since he cast Smith in *Weird Science* and later Eric Stoltz and Lea Thompson in *Some Kind of Wonderful* and even Ben Stein (who would go on to utter the iconic line, "Bueller?... Bueller?..." in *Ferris Bueller's Day Off*).

The memorable theme song "Weird Science" was composed by Danny Elfman of Oingo Boingo. John Hughes, known for his affinity for New Wave music, personally reached out to Elfman to create the song. Unlike Simple Minds with *The Breakfast Club*, Elfman was all in and composing music in his head while speaking to Hughes on the phone driving through Los Angeles, rushing to record it as soon as he got home. According to him, he had to be careful not to turn on the radio or hear any other song or he would have lost it in his head. Apparently Elfman's car was among his most inspirational place, as he wrote the theme to *The Simpsons* there as well.

Elfman recalls in an October 27, 2014, interview with *AV Club* magazine that "it was a goof to do and I wanted to do it for fun, and John was a nice guy." The song, which features a sample from *The Bride of Frankenstein*, became Oingo Boingo's most famous track, appearing both on the *Weird Science* soundtrack and their album *Dead Man's Party*. Despite its popularity, Elfman later disowned the song, feeling it was too "poppy"; he was further disheartened after the music video was mocked on *Beavis and Butt-Head*.

Weird Science premiered on August 2, 1985, just six months after *The Breakfast Club*. It debuted at number four at the box office, ironically trailing behind *National Lampoon's European Vacation*, the film Hall had turned down. With a budget of $7.5 million, *Weird Science* grossed $23 million, not a blockbuster hit but enough to solidify its status as a cult classic over the years, eventually adding another $20 million to its earnings.

In 1994, *Weird Science* was adapted into a television series by St. Clare Entertainment, a Universal subsidiary run by John Landis, in partnership with USA Network. The series, which lasted five seasons with eighty-eight episodes, closely followed the film's plot, with model Vanessa Angel playing the role of Lisa. In the pilot Gary refers to the original film, claiming that creating Lisa is possible because he "saw it in a John Hughes movie." Danny Elfman's theme song was also used in the series, although he wasn't credited on screen. John Hughes had no involvement in the show and was reportedly surprised when he discovered it, having mistaken it for a rip-off before realizing it was an adaptation of his own work. As he remarked in an interview, "I was sitting at home, watching TV, and this commercial comes on for this new show. I'm watching it, thinking 'Jesus, they ripped me off. This looks just like *Weird Science*.' Imagine my surprise."

The combined box office success of *The Breakfast Club* and *Weird Science* amassed almost $70 million, which marked 1985 as the year John Hughes firmly established his place in Hollywood. Yet it was just the beginning of what would become an even more impressive career.

6

Pretty in Pink

John Hughes was known for his intense dedication to his work, and he could be difficult to work with if he felt that others didn't share his passion or appreciate his vision. This intensity was evident during the production of *The Breakfast Club*. When he screened a rough cut of the film for Universal executives, their lukewarm reaction prompted Hughes to seek an exit from his deal with the studio. Despite having two successful films in 1985—*The Breakfast Club* and *Weird Science*—by the end of the year, Hughes decided to move on and signed a deal with Paramount Pictures, where his pal Ned Tanen had just become President after leaving Universal.

During this time, Hughes was particularly fond of working with Molly Ringwald, whom he saw as a muse. Between writing *Sixteen Candles* and *The Breakfast Club*, he penned *Pretty in Pink* specifically for her. Hughes also had a strong creative bond with Anthony Michael Hall, and both actors were central to his vision of the teenage experience. The roles of Andie Walsh and Phil "Duckie" Dale in *Pretty in Pink* were written with Ringwald and Hall in mind. However, both actors turned down the project, feeling that it was too similar to their previous work in *Sixteen Candles*. Hall, in particular, feared being typecast, stating that, "The girl wants the handsome kid, and the dorky kid is after her. To me, it was replicating *Sixteen Candles*."

Hughes felt betrayed by both actors. Molly Ringwald's rejection of the role was especially painful for him, as she had not only inspired the film but had also suggested the title. She introduced Hughes to the band The Psychedelic Furs and their song "Pretty in Pink," which became the movie's namesake. The character of Andie Walsh was deeply intertwined with Ringwald's own personality, down to the pink color that was her favorite and the bedroom in the film that resembled her own in real life.

Hughes's feelings of being betrayed by both actors led him not to direct *Pretty in Pink* himself. Instead, he passed the directorial baton to Howard Deutch, a music video director who had previously worked on movie trailers, including one for *Sixteen Candles*. Deutch had never directed a feature film before. In fact it was Deutch's father, Murray Deutch, who, as the president of United Artists Records, got his son jobs directing the music videos for Billy Idol's "Flesh for Fantasy," Billy Joel's "Keeping the Faith" and Stan Ridgway and Stewart Copeland's "Don't Box Me In," for Francis Ford Coppola's film *Rumble Fish*. However, Deutch also had a background in advertising like Hughes, so the two quickly bonded.

At the time, Hughes was ready to transition from directing to building a more substantial film production empire. The moderate success of *Sixteen Candles*, *The Breakfast Club*, and *Weird Science* in 1985 had established him as a significant figure in Hollywood, but the films were not yet considered iconic. Hughes wanted to focus on writing and producing, allowing others to direct his scripts. *Pretty in Pink* would be the first test of this new approach.

Hughes was beginning to realize that he could start doing multiple projects at once if he had someone else to direct, so he actually offered Deutch the choice between directing *Pretty in Pink* or another script he had written entitled, *The New Kid*. The latter was a more personal story based on Hughes's own experiences of moving around frequently as a child, focusing on a teenager adjusting to a new high school in Arizona. Deutch chose *Pretty in Pink*, and despite his lack of experience in directing feature films, Hughes was confident in Deutch's abilities and promised to be available around the clock for any guidance he might need.

However, Paramount, which was now producing *Pretty in Pink*, was hesitant to entrust the project to a first-time director. The studio preferred a more experienced filmmaker, but Hughes insisted on Deutch. Deutch later recalled in an interview with *Forbes* that during a dinner at Hughes's house, they received a call from Dawn Steel, head of production under Paramount's president, Ned Tanen. Steel was pushing for a more experienced director, but Hughes stood by Deutch, determined to give him the opportunity to direct the film.

Paramount eventually agreed to give Howard Deutch the green light for *Pretty in Pink*, but they allocated a modest budget of $7 million. This relatively low figure indicated the studio's lack of confidence in Deutch, such that even if the film didn't perform well, they wouldn't face significant losses.

The first major task for Deutch was to cast the lead role of Andie, especially since Molly Ringwald had initially declined the part. Jennifer Beals, fresh from her success in *Flashdance*, was the first choice. However, Beals, wary of being typecast as a high-school student, chose to focus on her college education instead. Other actresses considered included Jodie Foster, Sarah Jessica Parker, and Tatum O'Neal. Despite the tension between Ringwald and Hughes, Deutch insisted that she was perfect for the role, given that it had been written specifically for her. Eventually, Ringwald agreed to return as Andie.

For the role of Blane, Hughes initially wanted Charlie Sheen, whom he later cast in *Ferris Bueller's Day Off*. However, with Ringwald back in the lead, she felt she should have a say in who would play her on-screen love interest. After watching *St. Elmo's Fire*, she recommended Andrew McCarthy, who ultimately landed the part.

The casting of Duckie, a role originally intended for Anthony Michael Hall, was another point of contention. Ringwald pushed for Robert Downey Jr., but Deutch saw Jon Cryer as the perfect fit after his audition and chose him instead. Cryer's performance would later become one of the film's most memorable elements.

James Spader was cast as Steff, Blane's wealthy and arrogant friend, despite Deutch's initial reservations. Spader's audition was so convincing that Deutch found him unpleasant, even noting how Spader crushed a cigarette on his way out fully embodying the character. Deutch wanted to reject him, describing him as "terrible" and "mean." According to Deutch, Hughes said to him, "What's wrong with you? That's the character."

Filming for *Pretty in Pink* began on June 22, 1985, and wrapped on October 12, 1985, in Los Angeles. The high school scenes were shot at John Marshall High School, the same location used for the movie musical *Grease*.

Although John Hughes served as the writer and executive producer, fulfilling his promise to be available for Deutch, he kept his distance from Molly Ringwald on set. This strained relationship was difficult for Ringwald, who later expressed how hurtful it was that Hughes avoided interacting with her during the production. This lingering tension cast a shadow over their once close creative partnership, with Ringwald remarking, "It was very hurtful, and it still hurts."

One of the most memorable scenes in *Pretty in Pink* is Duckie's iconic lip sync of "Try a Little Tenderness" by Otis Redding. Interestingly, the original script only specified, "Duckie comes in lip-synching a song with great energy." Jon Cryer initially proposed lip-syncing the Mick Jagger and Michael Jackson duet "State of Shock." This song, originally intended as a duet between Jackson and Freddie Mercury for *Thriller*, was later recorded for The Jackson's *Victory* album with Jagger. However, when that idea didn't pan out, Hughes and Deutch considered using "Start Me Up" by the Rolling Stones, but they couldn't secure the rights.

Ultimately, it was Deutch who discovered the Otis Redding track, believing it perfectly encapsulated Duckie's heartbreak and unrequited love for Andie. Deutch explained, "It needed to be a heartbreaking song that would express just how Duckie felt–how hurt he is and how much he's in love with this woman. And we fall in love with him because we all relate to that." The day before filming, Deutch connected Cryer with choreographer Kenny Ortega to work on the scene. Not expecting it to become such an iconic moment, Deutch was so impressed with what Cryer and Ortega had created that the production schedule was extended to ensure the scene was captured in its entirety. Today, it's considered one of the best musical scenes ever filmed.

Over the years, another intriguing detail has emerged regarding the film's original ending, as written by John Hughes. Initially, Andie was supposed to end up with Duckie. Deutch recalled that "the first test screening had been like a rock concert, then we go to the ending and the people rose up and started booing." The reaction was especially strong among the girls, who wanted Ringwald's character to "get the cute boy." In response, Hughes quickly wrote a new five-page ending, a rare move in the romantic comedy genre, defying the typical underdog-love-prevails narrative. The crew had just one day to reshoot the entire final scene. By then, Andrew McCarthy was in New York preparing for his Broadway role in *The Boys of Winter* with Ving Rhames and Wesley Snipes, and he had already cut his hair. As a result, McCarthy had to wear a wig for the entire final scene. To soften the blow for Duckie's character, a new love interest was introduced, played by Kristy Swanson of *Buffy the Vampire*. According to Deutch, Hughes said, "We have to protect Duckie's character here. We have to get him a Duckette." This is why Swanson is listed as Duckette in the credits.

Although the revised ending made the film more commercially successful, it troubled Hughes, leading him to eventually create the ending he originally envisioned in *Some Kind of Wonderful.*

The *Pretty in Pink* soundtrack is also notable for its cohesive feel, despite not including all the songs featured in the movie. In 1986, David Anderle, A&M's director of film music, told the *Los Angeles Times* on January 12, 1986, that "The soundtrack sounds like a legitimate album, not a compilation. You almost get the feeling that it could be all songs by one band, just with a lot of different lead singers." Unlike *The Breakfast Club*, where the title was independent of the film's famous song, *Pretty in Pink* was named after a 1981 song by the Psychedelic Furs. For the film, the band re-recorded the track, placing greater emphasis on the saxophone and polishing it for the soundtrack. Similar to Simple Minds' "Don't You (Forget About Me)," "Pretty in Pink" became the Psychedelic Furs' biggest U.S. hit.

Despite the lyrics "Isn't she pretty in pink?"—which might lead the audience to associate the song with Andie, especially when she wears her self-made pink prom dress—the song's meaning was originally quite different. Richard Butler, the band's lead singer, once explained that John Hughes misunderstood the song's intent. "It was actually about an unfortunate girl who is naked," Butler clarified. "It was a metaphor."

A song that was specifically written for the movie is the now legendary "If You Leave" by Orchestral Manoeuvres in the Dark (OMD). John Hughes, who was on the cutting edge of the "second" British invasion, was already familiar with OMD, even though they were not yet widely known in the U.S. When Hughes approached the band's founding members, Andy McCluskey and Paul Humphreys, to write a song for *Pretty in Pink*, they were thrilled and flattered, unlike Simple Minds, who had been hesitant to contribute to *The Breakfast Club* soundtrack. Hughes invited McCluskey and Humphreys to Paramount Studios in Hollywood, where they met him, Molly Ringwald, and Jon Cryer for the first time. Hughes explained that they were looking for a song to accompany the film's climactic prom scene.

McCluskey and Humphreys returned home and composed a song they were proud of, titled "Goddess of Love." Hughes loved it too. However, when the film's original ending—where Andie ends up with Duckie—was changed following the test screening, Hughes informed McCluskey that "Goddess of Love" no longer fit the new conclusion. He asked them to write a different song for the revised ending. With only two days to complete this task before heading out on a two-month tour with the Thompson Twins, and without their instruments (which had already been shipped to San Francisco), the duo found themselves under immense pressure. Adding to the pressure was that A&M Records was building a promo campaign around the band appearing on the latest John Hughes movie soundtrack, a soundtrack they still did not have a song for yet.

They worked late into the night at a Los Angeles studio, with Humphreys on the piano and McCluskey hurriedly scribbling lyrics. By four o'clock, they had produced a rough demo, which they recorded onto a cassette and sent to Paramount Pictures. Just five hours later, their manager called to relay that Hughes loved the song and wanted them to return to the studio to finish it. The result was "If You Leave," which became the iconic track that closes the film. Interestingly, since the new song wasn't ready in time, the prom scene was initially shot to the tune of "Don't You (Forget About Me)."

The *Pretty in Pink* soundtrack became a huge success, reaching number five on the Billboard charts. To underscore how seriously John Hughes took the music in his films, he even wrote a rare director's note on the back cover of the album:

> The music in "*Pretty in Pink*" is not an afterthought. The tracks on this album and in this film are there because Howie Deutch and I believe in the artists, respect the artists, and are proud to be in league with them.

Curiously, the band The Rave-Ups, who appear in the film performing two songs, do not feature on the soundtrack album.

On August 29, 2013, *Rolling Stone* ranked *Pretty in Pink* eleventh on their list of the top twenty-five soundtracks of all time (with The Beatles' *Help!* at number one).

Released on February 28, 1986, *Pretty in Pink* was the highest-grossing movie of March that year, ultimately earning $40 million on a $9 million budget. It was another hit for John Hughes, and 1986 was just the beginning of a big year for him.

7

Ferris Bueller's Day Off

"I want to make a movie about a kid who takes a day off from school and... that's all I know so far," John Hughes told his friend and then-President of Paramount Studios, Ned Tanen, on February 25, 1985. *The Breakfast Club* had just been released on February 15, 1985, and while *Weird Science* had yet to open, the strong reviews for *The Breakfast Club* had Hughes eager to keep creating while he was still relatively young.

Tanen, a long-time supporter of Hughes, was on board with whatever idea Hughes had in mind. However, a looming writers' strike was set to begin on March 5, 1985, leaving Hughes with a very tight deadline.

True to form, Hughes, the prolific writer, churned out the script in record time. Not only would he write movie scripts in a week or a long weekend but he would actually write his progress day by day. This is the progress for the screenplay of *Ferris Bueller's Day Off*: ten pages on February 26th, twenty-six pages on the 27th, nineteen pages on the 28th, nine pages on March 1st, twenty pages on March 2nd, and the final twenty-four pages on March 3rd. By March 4th, just a day before the writers' strike began, the script for *Ferris Bueller's Day Off* was complete, and the project was greenlit the next day. The strike itself lasted only two weeks that year, but Hughes had already secured his next film.

While Hughes and Howard Deutch were working on *Pretty in Pink*, Deutch, who was staying with Hughes, recalled how Hughes handed him the first fifty pages of *Ferris Bueller's Day Off* early one morning after a night of writing. Deutch, having fallen asleep on Hughes's couch at midnight, was woken at five-thirty in the morning by blasting music and a chain-smoking Hughes. According to Deutch, the pages were so good that they barely needed any revisions.

Unlike Hughes' previous films, which were primarily set in the Chicago suburbs, *Ferris Bueller's Day Off* was intended to capture the essence of Chicago itself. Hughes wanted to focus not only on the architecture and landscape but also on the spirit of the city.

Although Ferris Bueller was not based on a real person, like many of Hughes's films, he was inspired by his own high-school experiences. In August 2009, however, Edward McNally, an attorney and former President Bush administration official, wrote an article for *The Washington Post* suggesting that he may have been the inspiration for Ferris Bueller. McNally, who attended the same high school as Hughes, claimed to have had a best friend named Buehler who engaged in similar antics, including accumulating twenty-seven absences (compared to Ferris's nine), being pursued by the school dean for forged sick notes, and attempting to erase extra miles on his father's purple Cadillac El Dorado by running the car in reverse—though in McNally's case, it accidentally shaved off 10,000 miles instead of ending in disaster. McNally's story was published three days after Hughes's death, leaving the true inspiration behind Ferris Bueller a mystery.

Hughes has always insisted that he envisioned Matthew Broderick as Ferris from the start, but this claim is a bit contested. Anthony Michael Hall suspected that Hughes originally wrote the role with him in mind. Alan Ruck, who ultimately played Ferris' best friend, Cameron Frye, mentioned that Hall was indeed offered the part but turned it down. Johnny Depp, during his appearance on *Inside the Actors Studio*, claimed that he was offered the role of Ferris Bueller but had to decline in order to work on *Platoon* with Oliver Stone (incidentally, working on *Platoon* didn't prevent Charlie Sheen from making a cameo in *Ferris Bueller's Day Off*). Eric Stoltz, before being cast in *Some Kind of Wonderful*, also auditioned for the role of Ferris.

Ultimately, Matthew Broderick landed the role, reportedly after Hughes saw him in the 1985 medieval fantasy film *Ladyhawke* (the film that Emilio Estevez tried to score tickets for by using his stardom, thereby inspiring the "Brat Pack" moniker), which premiered in April 1985, two months after the *Ferris Bueller* script was written. However, considering the nod to Broderick's 1983 movie *Wargames* in *Ferris Bueller*, it's clear that Hughes was already aware of Broderick's talents when writing the script. Mia Sara, who played Ferris's girlfriend, was cast after Hughes saw her performance in an advance screening of the 1985 fantasy film *Legend*, where she co-starred with Tom Cruise under the direction of Ridley Scott.

Jeffrey Jones, who took on the role of Principal Rooney, was cast based on his performance in the award-winning movie *Amadeus*. Hughes felt that Jones's portrayal of the emperor in *Amadeus* would lend itself well to playing the authoritarian principal. Hughes has mentioned that the character of Edward Rooney was inspired by his own Vice Principal from Glenbrook North High School.

Alan Ruck's character, Cameron, was based on a real friend of Hughes from high school. Cameron's decision to wear a Detroit Red Wings jersey throughout the movie, despite the Chicago setting, has multiple explanations. First, Hughes, as a lifelong hockey fan and Michigan native, grew up rooting for the Red Wings, particularly his childhood hero Gordie Howe (hence the number nine on Cameron's jersey). Even after adopting Chicago as his home and becoming a Blackhawks season-ticket holder, Hughes never fully abandoned his childhood team. Alternatively, Hughes has said the jersey is Cameron's "own quiet act of defiance, a way to express his inner rebellion." Alan Ruck offered another explanation, revealing that a cut plot point explained that Cameron had a close relationship with his grandfather, who used to take him to Red Wings games, and the jersey was a sentimental reminder of those cherished times.

After the release of *Ferris Bueller's Day Off*, according to Hughes' son, Gordie Howe reached out to John Hughes to express his appreciation for the nod to his legacy. He even sent Hughes a photo of himself wearing a shirt that read, "Leisure Rules, Ferris Bueller's Day Off," with the number nine—his iconic jersey number—drawn across the midsection.

The iconic performance of Ben Stein as the monotone economics teacher came about in a roundabout way. Stein has recounted that it was Richard Nixon who first introduced him to *New York Times* columnist Bill Safire. Safire then introduced Stein to an executive at Warner Brothers, who in turn connected him with a casting director. That casting director eventually introduced Stein to John Hughes. Stein has noted that Hughes's decision to cast him in the movie was because he and Hughes were the only Republicans in the entertainment business at the time. Hughes later explained that, while Stein wasn't a professional actor, his flat voice and unassuming appearance made him a natural choice for the role. Originally, Stein was supposed to deliver his lines off camera, but the student extras on the set found his deadpan delivery so amusing that Hughes decided to film him. Stein came up with the lecture topic of supply-side economics on his own after Hughes asked him to speak on a subject he knew well. The cast and crew broke into applause after Stein successfully delivered his lines with the "boring" monotone Hughes had envisioned. The now famous "Bueller?... Bueller?..." line was, however, part of the original script.

Jennifer Grey was cast as Ferris's sister after Hughes saw her in *Red Dawn* (in which she starred alongside Patrick Swayze, before reuniting for *Dirty Dancing*). According to Hughes, Grey came in for an audition, and they quickly began playfully insulting each other. Hughes jokingly remarked that he was glad her character was the first to be killed in *Red Dawn*. Grey's quick wit and banter impressed Hughes so much that he hired her on the spot without having her read a scene. He later described Grey as having a "charmingly obnoxious" quality that made her perfect for the role.

John Hughes had a unique approach to rehearsals, insisting on a period where the actors spent time together and visited the film's locations. Since *Ferris Bueller's Day Off* would prominently feature Chicago, Hughes took the principal cast—Matthew Broderick, Alan Ruck, Mia Sara, and Jeffrey Jones—around the city during their rehearsals, which began on August 29, 1985. The group was staying in the same Chicago hotel, and Hughes would meet with them in the same room every day.

Jones recalled a day where they were out driving in a Lincoln Town Car, "John was driving and I was sitting in the passenger seat, and Matthew and [costars] Alan Ruck and Mia Sara were sitting in the back seat. And he was slamming cassettes into the dash, saying this is the music we're going to use for—[he'd describe a scene]." Jones continued, "He was showing us Highland Park, which was where he was from. He was explaining to the four principal actors that he was still searching for the music for the big parade sequence." Hughes is quoted as saying, "I want something like Elvis or the Beatles but then I want something Midwestern kind of schmaltzy." It was Jones who suggested Wayne Newton, specifically the song "Danke Schoen," calling it the "schmaltziest" thing ever. Hughes, unfamiliar with Newton's work, immediately stopped at a music store and bought a Wayne Newton cassette. During the same stop, Jones found some flip-up sunglasses, which Hughes thought were perfect for the film, so he bought three pairs.

John Hughes used the rehearsal process as a way to get to know his actors, which was crucial for his films. His familiarity with the cast often led him to rewrite scenes on the fly, tailoring dialogue and actions to suit the actors' strengths and personalities. Hughes was known for his high shooting ratios, a rarity in the 1980s. It's estimated that he shot over a million feet of film for *Ferris Bueller's Day Off*, of which about 650,000 were printed. While such extensive filming is more common today, it was unusual in 1985.

Principal photography for *Ferris Bueller's Day Off* began in Chicago on September 9, 1985. Hughes noticed that Chicago residents were often annoyed by his filming in the city. He once said, "The more people who get upset with the fact that I film there, the more I'll make sure that's exactly where I film." This rebellious attitude might explain why he was so adept at capturing the spirit of high schoolers in his movies. Hughes was not only focused on making a great film but also on showcasing Chicago in a romantic light. He wondered why no one ever questioned Woody Allen for always filming in New York.

The baseball scenes at Wrigley Field were filmed on September 24, 1985, during a Cubs vs. Montreal Expos game. However, the game that Principal Rooney watches on TV while at the pizza place is actually from June 5, 1985, when the Cubs played the Braves. The Braves and Expos wore similar-looking road jerseys that season, so the difference went unnoticed by most viewers. Some bloggers have speculated that Ferris Bueller's actual day off was June 5, based on the game shown on TV.

The now legendary parade scene was filmed on September 28, 1985, at 230 S. Dearborn St., during the Von Steuben Day Parade, an annual German-American celebration honoring Baron Friedrich von Steuben, a Prussian general who helped train American troops during the Revolutionary War. The scene was actually filmed over two Saturdays. On the first Saturday, Hughes capitalized on the real parade, capturing authentic shots of the celebration. In the DVD commentary, Hughes revealed that the event organizers were unaware of his plans, allowing him to sneak a float into the parade for Matthew Broderick to sing on.

For the following weekend, they needed to recreate a fake parade. John Hughes reached out to local radio stations, asking them to announce an opportunity for people to appear in a John Hughes movie. After the success of *The Breakfast Club*, this excited a lot of locals, and reportedly around 10,000 people showed up.

A huge Beatles fan, Hughes listened to *The White Album* every day for fifty-six days during filming. He was determined to include their version of "Twist and Shout" in the movie, reportedly paying around $100,000 for the rights. Hughes's love for John Lennon also influenced other details in the film, such as the frequent appearance of the number nine. Cameron's Detroit Red Wings jersey bears Gordie Howe's number nine, and Ferris is absent for nine days. Hughes even mentioned that when Jeffrey Jones said "nine," it sounded particularly amusing. However, not everyone found it funny—Paul McCartney criticized the film for overdubbing "lousy brass" onto "Twist and Shout," remarking, "If it had needed brass, we'd have stuck it on ourselves!" Hughes was upset by McCartney's reaction but explained in the DVD commentary that, "We saw a band onscreen, and we needed to hear the instruments."

Kenny Ortega, who had previously choreographed the 1980 film *Xanadu* and Duckie's "Try a Little Tenderness" scene in *Pretty in Pink*, was brought in by Hughes not only to choreograph the parade scene but also to act as the second-unit director. Hughes's mentorship would eventually lead to Ortega's directing films like *Newsies and Hocus Pocus*, and TV shows like *Ally McBeal*, *Chicago Hope*, and the phenomenon *High School Musical*. Ortega described filming the parade scene as more like directing the Olympics than a movie, saying, "You've got all these thousands of people and one shot to get it right." Unfortunately, the choreography he and Matthew Broderick had prepared for the parade scene was never used because Broderick injured his knee while filming the scene where he runs through backyards and makes a big jump over a fence.

The Chicago Art Institute had never been filmed before *Ferris Bueller's Day Off*, and Hughes admitted it was "a self-indulgent scene of mine." The museum was a place of "refuge" for Hughes when he was in high school, so it made sense for him to showcase the paintings that were his favorites at the same age Ferris and his friends were supposed to be. The scene also serves as a deeper exploration of Cameron's character. When Cameron stares at George Seurat's *A Sunday Afternoon on the Island of La Grande Jatte*, Hughes explains that as Cameron looks closer at the child in the painting, "the less he sees. But the more he looks at it, there's nothing there, and that's Cameron."

Producer Ned Tanen, a Ferrari collector, like the owner of the house in Highland Park, Illinois, where the iconic car scene was filmed, secured permission to use the location. Replica cars, known as "replicars," were made for the scene where the car crashes through the window. Hughes also included Easter eggs in car license plates that reference his other movies: Ferris's mom Katie's car, a 1985 Chrysler LeBaron Town & Country (similar to the 'Family Truckster' in *National Lampoon's Vacation*), has a plate that reads "VCTN" (for *Vacation*); Ferris' dad Tom's 1985 Audi 5000 shows "MMOM" (for *Mr. Mom*). Jeannie's 1985 Pontiac Fiero "TBC" (*The Breakfast Club*); and Principal Rooney's 1985 Plymouth Reliant K "4FBDO" (*Ferris Bueller's Day Off*); while the plate on Cameron's dad's Ferrari simply reads "NRVOUS."

In late October 1985, the production of *Ferris Bueller's Day Off* moved to Los Angeles. Several key scenes, including those set at Ferris's house, the final chase sequence, the police precinct, and Ed Rooney's office, were all filmed there.

Location scouts knocked on the door of 4160 Country Club Drive in Long Beach, California, and asked homeowner Jim Balkman if they could use his house for a new John Hughes movie. The production team made only a few modifications, such as drilling a hole in the fence for Principal Rooney to peer through, installing a doggie door for him to climb through, and adding a fake intercom for him to yell through.

The producers would compensate the Balkman family with an extra $1,000 after unplugging their refrigerator, which spoiled their food but was necessary because it made too much noise during shooting. In the film, the refrigerator even features some of Hughes's son's drawings from when he was six. Incidentally, the house number in the movie—2800—is the same as John Hughes' childhood home.

John Hughes was a huge music fan, and his movie soundtracks are often as popular as the films themselves. For example, The Dream Academy's cover of The Smiths' "Please, Please, Please, Let Me Get What I Want" in the Art Institute scene has become as iconic as OMD's "If You Leave" from *Pretty in Pink*. So, why isn't there a soundtrack album for *Ferris Bueller's Day Off*?

David Anderle, president of A&M's film music division in 1985, had a close and creative relationship with Hughes. Anderle had worked on the film music for *The Breakfast Club* and *Pretty in Pink*. With a background in the recording industry dating back to the 1960s, including work with Brian Wilson of the Beach Boys, Anderle had connections with both legendary and emerging artists. He even commissioned Robert Smith from The Cure to write instrumental music for the Art Institute scene, which was right in line with Hughes's taste.

Hughes was so passionate about his movie soundtracks and music in general that he wanted A&M to become his private record label, dedicated exclusively to his films. However, Anderle told Hughes this was impossible since A&M was a major record company. After refusing Hughes' request, Anderle was subsequently fired, much like Anthony Michael Hall and Molly Ringwald were when they wanted to pursue other projects. As a result, Hughes lost the rights to Robert Smith's song as well.

Editor Paul Hirsch noted that initial test screenings of *Ferris Bueller's Day Off* received negative feedback on the museum scene. This may have been due to the original music choice—a classical guitar solo played on an acoustic guitar—selected after John Hughes's fallout with A&M Records. Initially, the parade scene followed the museum scene, but because the parade was such a high point, it overshadowed what came after. The decision was made to change the sequence of events, placing the museum scene before the parade, and to replace the music. This re-edit was well-received by audiences.

After the breakup with A&M, and the disappointment of seeing his beloved classical guitar solo rejected by audiences, Hughes decided not to release a soundtrack for the film, almost in defiance of A&M, like a high schooler would do. Although the studio was eager to produce one, Hughes explained in a 1999 interview, "I thought, 'Would kids want '*Danke Schoen*' and '*Oh Yeah*' (by Plutone and Yello) on the same record?'" However, he did agree to release a limited edition 7-inch single featuring "Beat City" by Flowerpot Man, the track playing when Ferris, Cameron, and Sloan first drive the Ferrari into Chicago, and "I'm Afraid" by Blue Room, which plays when Cameron falls into the swimming pool. Hughes had 100,000 copies pressed and mailed them to members of his fan club.

In 2016, to commemorate the film's thirtieth anniversary, La-La Land Records released an official soundtrack that included thirty-five tracks, featuring Ira Newborn's complete score.

The opening and closing scenes of the movie, where Matthew Broderick breaks the fourth wall and talks directly to the camera, were filmed on the last day of shooting, November 22, 1985. The original cut of the film was two hours and forty-five minutes long, so many scenes had to be trimmed to bring the runtime down to a more typical comedy length of one hour and forty-three minutes.

Ferris originally had a younger brother and sister who were cut from the final version, though they do appear in the original trailer. Another deleted scene involved Ferris visiting a Chicago radio station and claiming he would be the first teenager in space; this was removed following the Space Shuttle Challenger disaster that occurred earlier that year. Additionally, a backstory for Charlie Sheen's character, including his name, Garth Volbeck, and a subplot involving his family, was also left on the cutting room floor.

Released on June 11, 1986, *Ferris Bueller's Day Off* was an instant commercial success, grossing over $70 million on a $5 million budget. It became the tenth highest-grossing film of 1986, just behind the Best Picture winner *Out of Africa*. *Pretty in Pink*, another Hughes film, was the twenty-second highest-grossing film that year, meaning John Hughes single-handedly earned Paramount Pictures $110 million in 1986.

The film was also a critical success, with many reviewers describing it as "life-affirming." Richard Roeper of the Chicago Sun-Times even called it "something of a suicide prevention film," noting that Ferris's mission was to show Cameron that "life can be pretty sweet if you wake up and embrace it." Roeper's admiration for the film is evident; his own license plate reads "SVFRRIS."

Matthew Broderick was nominated for a Golden Globe Award for Best Actor in a Motion Picture–Comedy or Musical for his role as Ferris Bueller, but the award ultimately went to Paul Hogan for *Crocodile Dundee*. Like *The Breakfast Club*, *Ferris Bueller's Day Off* became a cultural phenomenon, with Broderick reprising his iconic role in a Super Bowl car commercial in 2012. Broderick has acknowledged that the character of Ferris "has eclipsed everything" else he's done. The movie's influence is still felt in pop culture, such as Ryan Reynolds' homage in *Deadpool* (2016), where Deadpool, dressed in a bathrobe, tells the audience to go home after the end credits, and in *Spider-Man: Homecoming* (2017), where Peter Parker runs through people's yards, jumping over hedges and fences, while *Ferris Bueller's Day Off* plays in the background at a pool party.

In August 1990, a television series based on *Ferris Bueller's Day Off* was created by producer and screenwriter John Masius, though John Hughes was not involved. Jennifer Aniston starred as the character originally played by Jennifer Grey. The show was a flop and was canceled after just four episodes, despite thirteen episodes being produced. Interestingly, in September 1990, the Fox network premiered *Parker Lewis Can't Lose*, a series heavily influenced by *Ferris Bueller's Day Off*. That show, however, lasted for three seasons.

Although Broderick and Hughes reportedly did not get along particularly well on the set of *Ferris Bueller's Day Off*, they stayed in touch for a few years after the film's release and even discussed a possible sequel that would follow Ferris in college and his first job, though it never materialized. As of February 2024, Paramount has greenlit a spinoff titled *Sam and Victor's Day Off*. The film will take place over a single day and focus on the two parking attendants who "borrowed" Cameron's car and put all the additional mileage on it in the original movie.

8

Some Kind of Wonderful

In 1984, John Hughes was reluctantly forced to move his family to California to edit *The Breakfast Club*. This relocation upset him so much that he vented his frustration in an interview with Roger Ebert of the *Chicago Sun-Times*, after the *Chicago Tribune* referred to him as a "former" Chicagoan. Hughes had once remarked that he would never move to Hollywood, saying, "I worked until I was 29 at the Leo Burnett advertising agency, and then I quit to do this. This is a working city, where people go to their jobs and raise their kids and live their lives. In Hollywood, I'd be hanging around with a lot of people who don't have to pay when they go to the movies." Despite his initial resistance, the temporary California stay extended to four and a half years, though he always maintained his home in Northfield, Illinois, to ensure his family could enjoy a proper Christmas.

While editing *Pretty in Pink* in Los Angeles, Hughes and director Howard Deutch discussed their disappointment over the test audiences and the studio forcing them to change the ending so that Duckie and Andie did not end up together. Hughes was so upset by this that he decided to write a new screenplay that mirrored *Pretty in Pink*, but with the genders reversed and ensuring that the "Duckie" character would get the happy ending. Between September and December of 1985, Hughes wrote *Some Kind of Wonderful*. Determined to realize his vision, he approached Molly Ringwald and Andrew McCarthy to play the lead roles. However, Ringwald declined, stating in a 2010 interview with *The Atlantic*, "I declined because I felt like the script wasn't strong enough and was too derivative of the other films I'd already made with John," which infuriated Hughes. McCarthy also turned down the role, feeling, "it seemed like we just kept making the same movie again."

Some Kind of Wonderful would ultimately be the only film Hughes made that was truly set in Los Angeles. Although *Pretty in Pink* and *Ferris Bueller's Day Off* were also shot in Los Angeles, they were designed to appear as if they took place in a Chicago suburb. *Some Kind of Wonderful* did not follow this pattern.

Hughes had already envisioned the soundtrack for *Some Kind of Wonderful* before writing the script. As a tribute to the Rolling Stones, he named the characters after members of the band: Eric Stoltz's character, Keith, after Keith Richards; Mary Stuart Masterson's character, Watts, after drummer Charlie Watts; and Lea Thompson's character, Amanda Jones, after the Rolling Stones song, "Miss Amanda Jones." While the soundtrack did not feature any major hits like "Don't You Forget About Me" from *The Breakfast Club*, it became a must-have for music lovers who shared Hughes's taste, as it was dominated by UK indie music from bands like The Jesus and Mary Chain and Flesh for Lulu. The March Violets performed a cover of "Miss Amanda Jones" in the film and also appeared in the film performing another song from the soundtrack, "Turn to the Sky."

With the soundtrack already envisioned, John Hughes initially wrote *Some Kind of Wonderful* as an over-the-top comedy centered on a boy planning the most extravagant date ever with the most popular girl in school. The original concept was so grand that it even featured the U.S. Navy Blue Angels flying overhead during dinner. As Hughes was preparing to focus on two other projects, he suggested Howard Deutch direct the film, viewing it as an L.A. remix of *Pretty in Pink* with a different ending. Despite his success with *Pretty in Pink*, Deutch still felt inexperienced and unsure about casting.

Deutch started by directly contacting Michael J. Fox, who was the biggest box office star at the time following *Back to the Future*. However, this move landed Deutch in hot water with Fox's lawyers and agents for not following proper channels. Paramount then took the casting responsibilities away from Deutch, which left him frustrated. Shortly after, Deutch found himself on a flight seated next to legendary director Brian De Palma (*Carrie, Scarface*). Deutch shared his casting troubles, and De Palma advised him, "If you can't cast it, you shouldn't do it." Inspired by this advice from one of the "fab five" (Scorsese, Spielberg, Lucas, Coppola, and De Palma), Deutch informed Ned

Tanen, the head of Paramount, that he wasn't interested in directing the film if he couldn't cast it.

John Hughes didn't take this news well. Known for holding grudges, Hughes reacted by having Deutch's office door padlocked and asking him to leave the studio lot. Hughes cut ties with Deutch, just as he had with Molly Ringwald and Anthony Michael Hall when they declined to participate in his projects.

Martha Coolidge was then brought in to direct. Known for her success with *Real Genius* starring Val Kilmer, Coolidge had previously directed *Valley Girl*, a film with a similar premise to *Some Kind of Wonderful*. *Valley Girl* featured Nicolas Cage as an L.A. punk from Hollywood High who falls in love with a spoiled girl from the California Valley. Hughes admired Coolidge for beating the Hollywood "system" by not only being a successful female director in 1982 but also by transforming *Valley Girl* from a broad comedy into a film with the kind of sincerity found in most of Hughes's work.

Coolidge took on the project with a focus on developing the script to exclude the broad comedy elements. She also cast Eric Stoltz as Keith and Mary Stuart Masterson as Watts. Her choices for the other lead roles included Kim Delaney, known for her work on the soap opera *All My Children* and later for *NYPD Blue*, as Amanda Jones, and Kyle MacLachlan, who would go on to star in *Twin Peaks* and *Sex and the City*, as Hardy, Amanda's wealthy and unkind boyfriend.

Hughes began to rework the script for *Some Kind of Wonderful*, making it darker and more dramatic to align with Martha Coolidge's vision as the new director. This shift in tone was so significant that Eric Stoltz, cast as the lead, was instructed to get hair extensions and darken his hair to add an air of mystery to his character. According to Stoltz, Coolidge aimed to create a teen film that was as non-verbal and non-comedic as possible—a stark contrast to Hughes's natural talent for witty, comedic dialogue.

Although Hughes was accommodating Coolidge's approach, he began to feel uncertain about the direction the film was taking. It was during this period of doubt that Ned Tanen, the head of Paramount, reached back out to Howard Deutch. Given how unprofessionally Deutch had been dismissed—with his office door padlocked—Tanen had to be tactful. He initiated their conversation by asking Deutch if he had seen the 1973 French film *Day for Night*, a romantic comedy-drama directed by François Truffaut. The film, which won the Oscar for Best Foreign Film also earned Truffaut a Best Director nomination.

He ended up losing out to Francis Ford Coppola for *The Godfather, Part II*, and Truffaut became a worldwide legend among the upcoming directors during that time period. Steve Spielberg was such a fan that Truffaut was asked to play Claude Lacombe, the French government scientist in charge of UFO-related activities in the United States, in the movie *Close Encounters of the Third Kind*.

Deutch admitted he hadn't seen the film, so Tanen suggested he watch it and call him back. *Day for Night* chronicles the troubled production of a melodrama and the various personal and professional challenges faced by the cast and crew. After watching the film, Deutch called Tanen back and quipped, "That's the story of my life." Tanen agreed and then broached the real reason for his call: Hughes was unhappy with Coolidge's direction and wanted Deutch to return to the project.

Deutch was initially hesitant, as the film had already secured locations, hired a crew, and cast actors—all without his involvement. However, Hughes assured Deutch that if he returned, he would have complete creative control.

There was, of course, the issue that Martha Coolidge was still the director. Four days before shooting began, Hughes and Deutch met and reconciled. Coolidge later recounted in a 2011 interview, "John decided in a gesture of friendship to make the studio give the movie to Howard to direct." When Coolidge came in after the weekend to start filming, she was summoned to the office of executive producer Michael Chinich, who informed her that the film would proceed, but without her as the director. Hughes never spoke to her directly, but Ned Tanen apologized, and Paramount paid her full salary.

Upon returning, Deutch immediately focused on recasting. He wanted to replace Kyle MacLachlan and Kim Delaney, and he even considered firing Eric Stoltz. While he succeeded in replacing MacLachlan, the studio insisted on keeping Stoltz, likely to avoid another public relations disaster, with Stoltz having already been famously fired from *Back to the Future*.

Ironically, the call to Michael J. Fox, which had jeopardized Deutch's initial involvement with the film, came after Deutch had already reached out to Lea Thompson, also from *Back to the Future*, to offer her the role of Amanda Jones. Thompson initially turned down the role to star in *Howard the Duck*. Though it seems surprising in hindsight, *Howard the Duck* was expected to be a massive success, with George Lucas even stepping down as president of Lucasfilm to focus on the project. However, when *Howard the Duck* became a legendary box-office flop, Thompson contacted Deutch, begging for another chance to join *Some Kind of Wonderful*. Deutch accepted her back on the project.

Deutch was pleased with the way Hughes rewrote the script, transforming it from a broad comedy into a more nuanced romantic dramedy. Stoltz recalled Hughes's evolving feelings about the project, noting, "He seemed to like it, then he didn't like it, and fired most of the cast and Coolidge, and we began again, going back to the simpler idea of *Pretty in Pink* with the sexes reversed." After reading the revised script, Deutch realized that Stoltz would be a good fit for the role, especially since it was no longer primarily comedic—a factor that had led to Stoltz being let go from *Back to the Future*. Ironically, Stoltz and Thompson already had chemistry from their six months together on the set of *Back to the Future*, even if that project didn't work out for Stoltz. They had also previously worked together in *The Wild Life*, a sort of follow-up to *Fast Times at Ridgemont High*, written by Cameron Crowe.

Filming for *Some Kind of Wonderful* began on August 11, 1986, just two months after the release of *Ferris Bueller's Day Off*. Although Deutch was the director, Hughes's influence was pervasive, with him either on set or rewriting scenes from afar. For instance, when Keith is preparing for his big date with Amanda, Hughes felt the scene needed more impact and quickly wrote what Deutch described as "the kiss that kills." Deutch remembers this well because Hughes wrote the scene right in front of him in an hour and a half:

To help Keith prepare for his date with Amanda, Watts suggests he practice kissing her. He agrees, but their kiss nearly becomes something more as she wraps her legs around him and his hands dip lower into her back pockets, which the camera fluidly tracks.

One of the film's highlights is a pivotal scene set at the Hollywood Bowl, a location rarely used in movies at the time. The Hollywood Bowl, with its distinctive bandshell, had only been used a handful of times in the movies, mostly going back to the 1930s and 40s with *A Star is Born* and *Anchors Away*, as well as an episode of *Columbo* in the 70s. Deutch was thrilled to shoot there, but in a 2019 interview with *Entertainment Weekly*, he recalls the challenge of filming in such an enormous venue: "That was a difficult night, and it took all night. The Hollywood Bowl is enormous, and if you're going to shoot it, you've got to shoot it wide, medium, tight, tighter."

Unfortunately, the next morning Deutch was told the lab scratched all the film from that night, making a reshoot costly. Fortunately, Deutch was able to edit around the scratches and use the original footage.

Shooting wrapped in mid-October 1986, and *Some Kind of Wonderful* had its Hollywood premiere on February 23, 1987, with a theatrical release following on February 27. The film debuted in sixth place at the box office, overshadowed by *A Nightmare on Elm Street 3*, which was released the same day. It grossed only $18 million, a modest sum by Hughes' standards, and finished fifty-eighth for the year, far behind blockbusters like *Beverly Hills Cop II*, *Platoon*, and *Fatal Attraction*.

While Roger Ebert of the Chicago Sun-Times and Janet Maslin of *The New York Times* found the film entertaining, their reviews were not glowing. Maslin did, however, acknowledge it as a "much-improved, recycled version of the *Pretty in Pink* story." In hindsight, *Some Kind of Wonderful* has gained a more favorable reputation and is now considered a classic in Hughes' filmography, even if it doesn't quite reach the iconic status of *Sixteen Candles*, *The Breakfast Club*, or *Pretty in Pink*.

Some Kind of Wonderful would be Hughes's final teen-angst movie. As he matured, his work would continue to explore dramedy, but with more adult-oriented themes, even if the protagonists were often still young.

9

She's Having a Baby

With six written and four directorial successes under his belt, John Hughes reached a point in his career where he, like many directors, felt the need to share something personal with his audience. Similar to how Bob Fosse did with *All That Jazz* or Woody Allen with *Annie Hall*, Hughes wanted to give viewers a glimpse into his own life, but in a subtle way, allowing them to piece it together on their own. *She's Having a Baby* stands as the closest the audience will ever get to knowing John Hughes on a personal level.

Just before *Planes, Trains and Automobiles* broadened his image beyond the realm of teen dramedies, Hughes penned *She's Having a Baby*, a film that serves as a natural conclusion to his exploration of youth, marking the transition into adulthood.

One reason Hughes wasn't available to direct *Some Kind of Wonderful* was that he needed to helm this deeply personal project. In *She's Having a Baby*, Kevin Bacon's character, Jake, mirrors Hughes's own life. Like Hughes, Jake met his wife (played by Elizabeth McGovern) in high school and married young. Jake works as a copywriter at a Chicago advertising firm but dreams of becoming a creative writer, just as Hughes once aspired to write movies. The final shot of Jake's manuscript, titled "She's Having a Baby," reveals Hughes's subtle way of telling the audience that this story is about himself. The end credits even credit Hughes' wife, Nancy, as the movie's "inspiration."

Hughes once said that *She's Having a Baby* is "about discovering that getting married isn't like flipping a switch—you actually have to work at it to derive any satisfaction from it." The film explores Jake's journey as he waits for that switch to flip.

In addition to Bacon and McGovern, Hughes—as he often liked to do—brought back several adult actors he had worked with before, among them John Ashton (*Some Kind of Wonderful*), Paul Gleason (*The Breakfast Club*), and Edie McClurg (*Ferris Bueller's Day Off*), along with Alec Baldwin as Jake's best friend.

Hughes and Kevin Bacon spent significant time together to ensure Bacon could accurately capture Hughes's mannerisms and values. Howard Deutch noted that Bacon came remarkably close to embodying Hughes's behavior. Interestingly, while Jake in *She's Having a Baby* closely resembles Hughes as an adult, characters like Ferris Bueller and Duckie in *Pretty in Pink* also reflect aspects of Hughes's personality.

She's Having a Baby began filming in Chicago in September 1986 and wrapped in December 1986.

The ending of *She's Having a Baby* is often highlighted as one of the film's standout moments, featuring cameos from thirty-one actors and musicians who suggest baby names for the lead characters. These cameos include John Candy and Dan Aykroyd, filmed while they were working on Hughes's movie *The Great Outdoors*. Matthew Broderick also makes an appearance as his iconic character, Ferris Bueller. Other notable cameos include Harry Anderson, Dyan Cannon, Robert Hays, Amy Irving, Michael Keaton, Penny Marshall, Bill Murray, Ally Sheedy, and Magic Johnson. Musicians such as Belinda Carlisle, Stewart Copeland (who also composed the score for the movie), Olivia Newton-John, Roy Orbison, and Warren Zevon contribute to the lineup. Hughes even visited the set of *Cheers* to film cameos with Kirstie Alley, Ted Danson, Woody Harrelson, and John Ratzenberger, who were all part of the Paramount family at the time.

Unlike *Ferris Bueller's Day Off*, *She's Having a Baby* featured an original soundtrack that has become a classic in Hughes's filmography. It includes tracks from cutting-edge British bands that Hughes admired, such as Love and Rockets and Gene Loves Jezebel, as well as new songs from XTC and Everything but the Girl. The soundtrack is divided into a "he" side, representing the male character's uncertainties and eventual acceptance, and a "she" side, reflecting the female character's longing and impatience. The standout track is Kate Bush's "This Woman's Work," written specifically for the film.

Hughes approached Bush with the idea of creating a song that would resonate with the film's emotional climax, where the husband faces the possible loss of his wife during childbirth. After receiving a video of the scene, Bush composed the song in her home studio, crafting lyrics from the husband's perspective to align with the visuals. Bush later revealed that she aimed to write a song that would "make people cry." Despite being rushed to complete it in time for the film's release, the song has since become one of Bush's most acclaimed works. Though it didn't chart well in the U.S., it has been praised by critics and featured in other films and television shows, including *The Handmaid's Tale*. The song was also famously covered by Grammy winning artist Maxwell, whose rendition is considered by some to surpass the original.

As it turns out, Bush could have taken more time with the song, as the film's release was delayed. This happened because John Hughes caught Steve Martin's interest with a new pitch and script just as a director's strike was looming.

10

Planes, Trains and Automobiles

While working on *Some Kind of Wonderful*, John Hughes shared a story with a friend about an experience he had years earlier during his regular commutes from Chicago to New York. At the time, Hughes was a copywriter for the Leo Burnett advertising agency, frequently stopping in New York to work at *National Lampoon* on the company's dime. He recalled a particular Wednesday when he had a presentation at eleven in the morning in New York and planned to return to Chicago on a five o'clock flight that same evening. However, due to weather, all flights to Chicago were canceled that night, forcing him to stay in a hotel. The next day, a snowstorm in Chicago delayed his flight again, and after a series of reroutes to Iowa, Denver, and Phoenix, Hughes didn't make it back to Chicago until the following Monday. During this ordeal, he met an old salesman who had spent years on the road and knew exactly how to handle such situations. As Hughes recounted this story at various dinners—where he often fleshed out ideas—he eventually went home after one of those dinners and wrote the first sixty pages of what would become *Planes, Trains and Automobiles* in just six hours.

At the time, Hughes and Howard Deutch were working closely together, often pulling all-nighters at Hughes' house. Deutch would fall asleep, only to wake up to find Hughes had written fifty or sixty pages of *Ferris Bueller's Day Off* during the night, asking, "What do you think?" While Deutch was directing *Some Kind of Wonderful* and Hughes was preparing for *She's Having a Baby*, Deutch stumbled upon the first sixty pages of *Planes, Trains and Automobiles* in Hughes' office. Excited, Deutch told Hughes, "I want to do this," and Hughes agreed.

Bill Brown, the production manager on *Some Kind of Wonderful*, recalled having dinner with Hughes one Wednesday night when Hughes mentioned he had an idea for a new project. By the following Tuesday, Hughes had written the script, and Paramount had already greenlit the project, which was around September 1986.

Initially, Hughes envisioned Tom Hanks and John Travolta in the roles of Neal and Del, but Hanks was in the middle of filming *Big*, and Paramount was hesitant to cast Travolta, who by 1986 had become a box-office disappointment.

Once the script was greenlit and word spread that Hughes was making an adult-themed comedy, the first person to reach out to Paramount's head, Ned Tanen, was Steve Martin. Hughes had long admired Martin, describing him as the funniest man alive and comparing him to the rock-and-roll bands he idolized. To Hughes, Martin was the first real rock-and-roll comedian, filling arenas rather than small clubs. A meeting was quickly arranged, and when Martin visited Hughes's home to discuss the movie, the two got along incredibly well. Now that Steve Martin was on board, Hughes decided he would direct the movie himself instead of Deutch.

As for John Candy, Hughes was already enamored after meeting him in 1983 on the set of *Vacation*, where they were both credited with saving the film. The next time they met, according to Candy, was on the Universal lot, while Candy was filming *Brewster's Millions* with Richard Pryor, and Hughes was directing *Weird Science*. Hughes was excited to see him, and the two hit it off. Inspired, Hughes reportedly went home and wrote two scripts with Candy in mind. However, a producer allegedly told Hughes that Candy was difficult to work with, causing Hughes to shelve the scripts. Later, Candy claimed, they would discover "that producer was a jerk." So, when Hughes had the chance to cast Candy in his next film, he jumped at the opportunity. With both Steve Martin and John Candy on board, Hughes felt confident that his first adult-themed broad comedy would be a success.

Despite just finishing *She's Having a Baby* in December of 1986, Paramount had greenlit *Planes, Trains and Automobiles* with a looming directors' strike predicted by the end of June 1987. Paramount wanted the film in theaters by Thanksgiving, giving Hughes only nine months to shoot, edit, score, and complete the movie—an ambitious timeline, even for someone as prolific as Hughes.

In September 1986, Hollywood columnist Marilyn Beck wrote that "Paramount is so high on the script—and on Martin and Candy—that it already has targeted *Planes, Trains and Automobiles* as its major release for the holiday season next year." This put immense pressure on Hughes and the film's production, especially considering the original script was 145 pages long—much too lengthy for a comedy. When Steve Martin suggested trimming some scenes, Hughes seemed puzzled by the idea. Not only did Hughes refuse to cut any material, but he also continued to add more while filming. He frequently rewrote scenes, handed out new pages to Martin and Candy just before shooting, and even filmed entirely new scenes on the fly as ideas struck him.

Various assistants on set recalled how Hughes would sometimes disappear into the restroom, only to emerge with ten additional pages of script. Hughes also recognized that working with comic talents like Steve Martin and John Candy meant improvisation was key, which further extended the filming process. During a 1989 interview on *Later with Bob Costas*, Candy shared that he and Martin would often finish a scene, remain in character, and continue improvising because they never heard the word "cut." Hughes would initially stick to the script for the first take but then instruct Martin to follow the script while telling Candy to improvise, and vice versa. If a scene involved a third or fourth person, they would film it four different times, in four different ways, in addition to shooting close-ups and establishing shots.

As the movie fell weeks behind schedule, Candy and Martin eventually made a pact to stop ad-libbing to help the production stay on track.

Paul Hirsch, the editor of *Planes, Trains and Automobiles*, shared an interesting example of how John Hughes approached filming. He described the first scene where Neal and Del take a taxi to their first hotel. In the original script, this scene was only about a third of a page long, suggesting it should take around thirty seconds of screen time. However, Hughes shot the scene with at least nine different camera setups: a shot of the cab from the front, close-ups of the driver, close-ups of Neal and Del, two-shots showing both characters together, and more. Hirsch noted that while a thousand feet of film—a single reel's worth—typically lasts about eleven minutes, Hughes shot forty thousand feet of film for this cab scene alone, resulting in over six hours of footage.

Filming for *Planes, Trains and Automobiles* began in Buffalo, New York, on March 2, 1987, and lasted eighty-five days, which was extraordinary for a comedy, as most shoots typically take only forty days.

The film was initially supposed to be shot entirely in the Chicago area, but a lack of snowfall forced the production to relocate to Buffalo. The first day of shooting was the scene where Neal and Del's burnt-out car is pulled over by a state trooper, played by Michael McKean. Ironically, there was now too much snow and limited visibility, so they had to wait a day for the weather to clear. Martin later remarked that they were living the plot of the movie as they filmed, hopping from trains to planes to automobiles in search of snow. The production moved from Buffalo to Ohio to St. Louis in pursuit of snowy locations. The unpredictable weather inflated the film's budget, but the studio was so confident in the project that they allowed Hughes to do whatever was necessary.

While in St. Louis, Hughes and Candy took in a few St. Louis Blues hockey games after a filming day. On April 4, 1987, they were interviewed by the Blues' color commentator during a game against the Minnesota North Stars. Candy, ever the comedian, joked that they were chasing snow to complete the movie.

Because most travel companies didn't want to be associated with the film due to its premise, the studio had to rent a 20-mile stretch of railroad track and construct sets for the airline and car rental scenes. They also had to create fictitious names and logos for the travel companies featured in the movie. This was unusual since travel companies usually pay for product placement in films. As a result, the fictional railroad company in the movie is called "Contrack," a blend of Conrail and Amtrak.

While John Hughes was filming *She's Having a Baby* and preparing for *Planes, Trains and Automobiles*, he shared details about the latter project with Kevin Bacon. Bacon was so captivated by the idea that he begged Hughes for a role, even if it was just a small part. As a result, Bacon appears in the film's opening scene, competing with Steve Martin's character for a taxi in New York City. Though Bacon is credited as "Taxi Racer," it's widely believed he's reprising his character, Jake Briggs, from *She's Having a Baby*, as he's dressed in the same outfit. This cameo adds a layer of humor for the audience and cleverly foreshadows the series of misfortunes to come. The scene is also a nod to Bacon's 1986 role in the movie *Quicksilver*, where he races a cyclist as a taxicab passenger. Interestingly, in the scene where Neal's wife, played by Laila Robins, is watching TV while waiting for him to return home, she's watching a clip from *She's Having a Baby*, specifically a scene where Kevin Bacon and Elizabeth McGovern argue about having overnight guests.

One of the most memorable scenes in *Planes, Trains and Automobiles* is the rental car confrontation with Edie McClurg's character as the rental agent. The scene lasts only about a minute but contains nineteen uses of "fuck," eighteen by Martin and one by McClurg, earning the film its R rating. Though neither Hughes nor Martin was generally fond of excessive swearing, they both felt that this scene warranted it. In test screenings, audiences agreed, finding the scene relatable—expressing frustrations most people feel but would never actually verbalize in real life. Reflecting on the scene, Martin has said he has no regrets, calling it a classic moment. He recalls director Mike Nichols once advising, "In every movie you do, there should be a scene where you say to yourself, can we do that?" The rental car scene was that moment for Hughes and Martin.

Another iconic moment in the film is when Neal and Del wake up cuddling in a shared motel bed. John Candy, in a 1989 interview, recounted how "every time we got into that position, we'd start laughing. Then we'd settle down and see the cameras start shaking, everybody lost it." Hughes even played the song "I'm Back in Baby's Arms," featured in the movie, while they were filming, which only added to the hilarity. It was Candy who came up with the improvised, now famous, lines, "Where's your other hand?" "Between two pillows," "Those aren't pillows!"—none of which were in the original script.

The ending of *Planes, Trains and Automobiles* is a poignant tearjerker, but it underwent significant changes from the original screenplay. In the initial version, Neal takes the train home, only to find Del waiting at the station. An angry Neal demands to know why Del is following him, leading to Del's revelation that, since his wife's death, he clings to people during his travels to avoid feeling alone. This version didn't test well with audiences, who laughed at Del's speech, which wasn't meant to be funny; it also made them dislike Del's character.

Editor Paul Hirsch shared in a 2019 podcast that he crafted a new ending by repurposing footage Hughes had shot of Steve Martin on the train, without Martin's knowledge. Hughes had instructed the cinematographer to film Martin as he quietly prepared for the next scene, capturing the introspective expressions Hughes had been trying to evoke throughout the film. Though Hughes hadn't originally intended to use this footage, it became the basis for the final version of the ending, where Neal pieces together the possibility that Del's wife is deceased. Hirsch reversed the footage of the train leaving the station to make it look like Neal returned to find Del, trimming Del's speech to just key lines. This gave Neal a sense of compassion and removed the impression that Del had guilted him into bringing him home.

John Candy's performance in *Planes, Trains and Automobiles* marked a significant turning point in his career, thanks in large part to John Hughes. While audiences were already familiar with Candy's comedic talents, this film showcased his depth as a dramatic actor. During filming, Hughes and Candy formed a close friendship, though, sadly, it would be cut short.

Candy, much like his character Del, was beloved by everyone on set. His warmth and generosity shone through when, on March 30, 1987, he invited the entire crew—actors, producers, key grips, and more—to his hotel room to watch the Oscars, ordering room service for everyone. This gesture exemplified the kind of person Candy was and highlighted why Hughes was drawn to him, developing a bond that would last for the remainder of Hughes's life. Hughes, who often connected deeply with his younger actors, finally found a peer in Candy with whom he could share a similar rapport.

Filming for *Planes, Trains and Automobiles* wrapped on July 1, 1987, just in time to avoid the looming Directors Guild strike, which was ultimately averted at the last minute. The first cut of the film, however, was famously long—clocking in at three hours and forty-five minutes, longer than *Titanic*. Clearly, it needed significant trimming. In a 2022 *Vanity Fair* interview, Hughes's son mentioned that the motel sequence alone "existed as this kind of one-act play within the movie." Editor Paul Hirsch echoed this, explaining that, while the sequence was well-crafted, it caused the road film to stall for forty-five minutes early on.

Hughes began to remove substantial portions of the movie, cutting subplots that, while interesting, weren't missed in the final version. For instance, there was a storyline where Neal's wife, played by Laila Robins, doubted Del's existence, suspecting that Neal was inventing him to cover up an affair. Another scene that was cut involved Neal and Del being robbed in their motel room after Del shortchanged and insulted a pizza delivery boy, turning the theft into an act of revenge and Del into a less-than-sympathetic character.

In September, the film went through nine different recuts, each screened for preview audiences as the team searched for the right balance. What began as an almost four-hour comedy was ultimately trimmed down to a tight hour and thirty-three minutes. In a 2022 *Vanity Fair* interview, editor Paul Hirsch recalled telling John Hughes that the cuts represented twenty-eight days of shooting. Hughes, unfazed, simply shrugged and said, "You know, oh well."

The soundtrack for *Planes, Trains and Automobiles* was a bit unconventional and faced delays and contractual issues. When it was finally released, six weeks after the film's premiere, it featured a mix of rock, country, and pop—quite a departure from Hughes' typical New Wave-inspired soundtracks—reflecting his shift away from teen films.

Hughes and music supervisor Tarquin Gotch initially aimed for a country-influenced soundtrack. Gotch traveled to Nashville and recorded with artists like Steve Earle and Emmylou Harris, among others. However, test audiences responded poorly, saying, "We love the film but not the music; it's too hick and country." In the end, they managed to include a track by the Fine Young Cannibals featuring Steve Martin.

Curiously, the soundtrack does not include two of the film's most iconic songs. Ray Charles's "Mess Around," which John Candy's character sings while driving, as Steve Martin's character sleeps, is notably absent despite being one of the most memorable scenes—so much so that it was parodied in the Seth MacFarlane movie *Ted 2*.

Disputes between Paramount and various record companies also affected the inclusion of other key songs. John Hughes had originally enlisted Elton John to write a song with the hope of creating a hit similar to "Don't You (Forget About Me)" from *The Breakfast Club*. However, just two days before the recording session, Paramount demanded that the original song master become the property of the studio. Elton John's record company, Polygram, refused, and the deal fell through. As a result, Hughes collaborated with David Steele and Andy Cox from the English band The Beat to create what became known as the love theme for the film, titled "I Can Take Anything."

Another legendary song from the movie is Paul Young's version of "Everytime You Go Away," which, like "Mess Around," didn't make it onto the official soundtrack. Young faced a similar issue to Elton John, as his record company denied the rights, despite approval from Young and the song's original writer, Daryl Hall from Hall & Oates. While the song does appear in the film, it's not performed by Paul Young but by Blue Room, a New Wave band from England that Hughes admired and had featured in previous movies. Blue Room's songs, like "I'm Afraid" from *Ferris Bueller's Day Off* and "Cry Like This" from *Some Kind of*

Wonderful, were among the tracks Hughes sent to fans as forty-fives in lieu of official soundtracks, and they ultimately recorded "Everytime You Go Away" for *Planes, Trains and Automobiles*.

In 2019, actor Ryan Reynolds, a devoted fan of *Planes, Trains and Automobiles*, posted a video on Twitter to honor the late John Candy, using Paul Young's original recording of "Everytime You Go Away" as the background music. Paul Young responded on Twitter, expressing his long-held disappointment: "I was so disappointed and deflated when my damn record company wouldn't let my version be used in *Planes, Trains and Automobiles*, so thank you, Ryan Reynolds, for finally using it in this lovely tribute to John!" Reynolds quickly replied, "This song still punches me in the heart every time. Thank you, Paul." To which Young responded, "Thanks, Ryan, that was my big moment to be in a movie with two heroes of mine, and CBS stabbed me in the heart over some tit-for-tat argument with Warner Brothers."

In 2021, Reynolds learned about the issues Elton John faced with his song for the film, and since then, he has been on the lookout for any existing version of the song that might have been recorded.

In 2024, Reynolds announced that he would be producing a documentary about John Candy. In September 2025, he premiered the finished film as the opening-night selection at the Toronto Film Festival. Its title, *John Candy: I Like Me*, is taken directly from Candy's famous hotel-room monologue in *Planes, Trains and Automobiles*.

Planes, Trains and Automobiles was released on November 25, 1987, to critical acclaim. The film was praised for Hughes's successful transition from teen comedies to more adult themes, and for the outstanding performances of Martin and Candy. Despite high hopes from Paramount, the film faced challenges at the box office. Rumors about its lengthy runtime began circulating two months before its release, and it only grossed $7 million in its opening weekend, finishing third behind *Three Men and a Baby* and the re-release of Disney's *Cinderella*. Although *Planes, Trains and Automobiles* eventually grossed $50 million on a $30 million budget, it ranked 21st in the box office for 1987, far behind the top-grossing *Three Men and a Baby*, which brought in $167 million despite having no major stars.

However, while *Three Men and a Baby* may have won at the box office, *Planes, Trains and Automobiles*, thanks to robust video sales, became a perennial favorite, especially during the holiday season on television. Over time, it not only gained cult status but also became recognized as a classic comedy.

There has long been speculation about the existence of a four-hour cut of the film. According to Hughes's sons, a VHS copy of this extended version existed, which Hughes would occasionally show to friends and those interested in filmmaking. To mark the film's thirty-fifth anniversary in 2022, Paramount released a 4K Blu-ray and video-on-demand edition that included over an hour of previously unseen footage thought to have been lost.

Since 2020, Paramount Pictures has been developing a remake of the film, with Kevin Hart and Will Smith attached to star. In 2023, Hart updated fans, mentioning that he was still working on the script, though this update came just before the infamous incident involving Will Smith and Chris Rock at the Oscars.

Meanwhile, during all the buzz surrounding *Planes, Trains and Automobiles*, Hughes had already completed his most personal film, *She's Having a Baby*, released by Paramount on February 5, 1988, less than three months after *Planes, Trains and Automobiles*. Unfortunately, the film received little attention and was both a critical and commercial failure, grossing only $16 million on a $20 million budget, making it the least successful film of Hughes's directing career. It ranked sixty-third at the box office for the year and didn't even make it into the top fifty video rentals of 1988.

Hughes was deeply disappointed by Paramount's treatment of *She's Having a Baby*, a film that meant so much to him. This experience led him to sever ties with the studio permanently in 1988 and found his own production company, Hughes Entertainment. According to a 1991 report in *Premiere* magazine, Paramount was left with a $750,000 bill for the renovations made to Hughes's office space at the studio.

11

The Great Outdoors

After leaving Paramount, Ned Tanen, the studio executive who had overseen hits like *Crocodile Dundee*, *Top Gun*, *Fatal Attraction*, and *Ferris Bueller's Day Off*, also resigned in November 1988, citing "burnout." Tanen had left Paramount on a high note, but with both Hughes and Tanen departing, the studio faced a downturn for a few years, making it a fitting time for Hughes to move on. In mid-1988, Hughes signed a new, non-exclusive deal with Universal Studios, marking his second stint with the studio.

After returning to Universal and searching for a new project, Hughes found himself thinking back to how he had previously mined his *National Lampoon* material—most notably when he turned "Vacation '58" into the script for *National Lampoon's Vacation*. During this second stint at the studio, he chose to adapt another piece from his Lampoon days: a short story titled "Fresh Air," published in the June 1980 issue. Originally written for the magazine's "real-life adventure" section with Ted Mann, the story offered a humorous take on outdoor misadventures, including a moment in which a character accidentally shoots an environmentalist. Hughes expanded that comic premise for what became the 1988 film *The Great Outdoors*, transforming it into a sequence where John Candy's character, Chet, inadvertently shoots a bear in the backside. Buoyed by the success of *Ferris Bueller's Day Off*, Universal agreed to finally greenlight this long-shelved idea.

Back in September 1986, when Paramount greenlit *Planes, Trains and Automobiles*, Howard Deutch was in the midst of directing *Some Kind of Wonderful*. Deutch was initially set to direct *Planes, Trains and Automobiles* as his next project. He completed *Some Kind of Wonderful* in October 1986 and began preparations for *Planes, Trains and Automobiles*. However, in early November, while Ned Tanen was still at Paramount, he informed Deutch that Steve Martin had signed on to the movie and mentioned that Hughes had a significant admiration for Martin. According to Deutch, in a 2022 *Vanity Fair* interview, Tanen hinted that Hughes might want to direct *Planes, Trains and Automobiles* himself but assured Deutch that Hughes had other projects in mind for him if that happened. Hughes eventually did decide to direct *Planes, Trains and Automobiles*, and the "other project" he had in mind for Deutch was directing *The Great Outdoors*.

After wrapping up *Planes, Trains and Automobiles* in July 1987, Hughes and Deutch offered John Candy the role of Chet in *The Great Outdoors*. Filming began on October 27, 1987, at Bass Lake, California, which stood in for the fictional Lake Potowotominimac in Pechoggin, Wisconsin. The role of Roman, Chet's brother-in-law, was initially offered to Chevy Chase, in an attempt to reunite Candy and Chase after their success in *National Lampoon's Vacation*. However, Chase was already committed to the film *Funny Farm*. Hughes then considered Bill Murray for the role, hoping to reunite him with Candy after their success in *Stripes*, but Murray was on a break from acting at the time. It was John Candy who suggested casting Dan Aykroyd, another Canadian native and long-time friend. Candy and Aykroyd had a history together, having first appeared in a children's sitcom in 1975 in Canada and later working together in Steven Spielberg's *1941* and John Landis' *The Blues Brothers*, where Aykroyd had hired Candy for a supporting role.

While Hughes was busy editing two films simultaneously—*She's Having a Baby* and *Planes, Trains and Automobiles*—he easily enlisted Howard Deutch to film a few scenes with Dan Aykroyd and John Candy, in character from *The Great Outdoors*, for the sequence at the end of *She's Having a Baby* where they humorously list possible baby names. As a result, John Candy appeared in three John Hughes movies within just seven months, solidifying his role as Hughes's new muse, much like Molly Ringwald had been in Hughes' earlier films.

As Hughes was growing increasingly discontented with Paramount and negotiating his deal with Universal while *The Great Outdoors* was in production, some scenes for the film were shot at the Paramount Ranch in the Santa Monica Mountains, a location used for hundreds of movies since the 1920s. Other scenes were filmed on the Universal backlot. Interestingly, the Loon's Nest vacation cabin, where Candy's character's family stays in the film, was a set on the Universal backlot—the same set used for "Bob's Country Bunker" in *The Blues Brothers*, which also starred Aykroyd and Candy.

Unlike most of Hughes's other films that he didn't direct, he only visited the Bass Lake set of *The Great Outdoors* a few times during filming and rarely interfered, except when script changes were necessary. Locals from the town noted that while Hughes would occasionally visit the set, he never disrupted the production. Instead, he often kept to himself at the bar-restaurant in Ducey's Lodge on the Lake, where much of the movie was set, despite being just as famous as John Candy and Dan Aykroyd at that time due to his string of hits.

According to Howard Deutch, he was unhappy during the production because Universal executives had insisted that John Candy shave the beard he had grown for his role, fearing it obscured too much of his face. Candy was upset by this request, as he felt the beard was integral to his character. Although Candy was a consummate professional, this decision dampened his spirits during filming.

Candy's good-natured personality made him a beloved figure on set, such that no one wanted to be the bearer of bad news. In fact, ten days before filming began, while in Bass Lake, Candy expressed a desire to watch the Tyson vs. Biggs fight. However, the town didn't have satellite or cable. To accommodate him, the owner of one of the local bars arranged for a limo to take Candy and his bodyguard to Fresno so they could watch the fight on TV.

Filming for *The Great Outdoors* took six weeks, wrapping up in December 1987. During production, the working title was "Big Country," but when Hughes learned that Tom Hanks' movie *Big* was set to release just nine days earlier, he realized the title needed to be changed. Universal then struck a deal with the well-known British magazine *The Great Outdoors*, the UK's leading authority on hill walking and backpacking. The magazine allowed the film to use its title, and the mock magazine cover became the movie's poster, with Dan Aykroyd holding up a fishing pole as if he had just "caught" John Candy as a fish.

As a gesture of appreciation, Hughes and Deutch held an early screening of the movie for the residents of Bass Lake, who had been welcoming and supportive during the production. Many of these locals can be seen in the final scene, dancing as the closing credits roll.

The soundtrack for *The Great Outdoors* deviates from the typical John Hughes musical style, though a few tracks have been included in the 2022 collection titled "Life Moves Pretty Fast–The John Hughes Mixtapes." The "Life Moves Pretty Fast" collection, curated by Hughes's long-time music supervisor Tarquin Gotch, spans Hughes's films from 1983 to 1989 and is available as a four-CD or six-LP red vinyl set.

The soundtrack for *The Great Outdoors* is unusual in that it features a mix of '80s electronic music and bluegrass. Dan Aykroyd and his Elwood Blues Revue contributed five tracks to the album, which also includes "Land of a Thousand Dances," the final song from the film, twice. Unfortunately, the soundtrack is currently out of print.

The Great Outdoors was released on June 17, 1988, just four months after the box-office disappointment of *She's Having a Baby* and five months before *Planes, Trains and Automobiles*, even though it was filmed afterwards. Grossing $43 million on a $24 million budget, the film was considered another disappointment for Hughes. It debuted in third place at the box office, trailing behind the Schwarzenegger action-comedy *Red Heat* (which, incidentally, takes place in Chicago and stars Jim Belushi, who would later work with Hughes multiple times) and the movie *Big*, then in its third week. *The Great Outdoors* ultimately ranked twenty-fifth for the year.

The reviews were equally underwhelming. Kevin Thomas of the *L.A. Times* headlined his review: "Candy, Aykroyd Wasted in *Great Outdoors*." He remarked that if John Hughes hadn't been the writer, it's hard to imagine the film getting made. While most critics panned the movie, they still praised the performances of Aykroyd and Candy. Peter Smith of the *Tampa Bay Times* noted, "John Hughes didn't have an idea for a summer film this year, but he went ahead and made one anyway." Hal Hinson of the *Washington Post* wrote, "If the John Candy-Dan Aykroyd comedy *The Great Outdoors* had a few more laughs, we might be tempted simply to write it off as mediocre and let it go at that. But this woodland farce is just coarse enough, and unfunny enough, to achieve true awfulness." *TV Guide* echoed the sentiment, stating, "Scripted by the extraordinarily prolific John Hughes, directed by Howard Deutch, and starring John Candy and Dan Aykroyd, this disappointing comedy should have been much funnier given the talent involved."

Critics also questioned the film's PG rating, given its swearing and some sexual innuendo—especially notable when compared to *Planes, Trains and Automobiles*, which received an R rating due to a single scene.

As of 2021, Dan Aykroyd, according to an interview he gave in *The Hollywood Reporter*, and Howard Deutch were considering a sequel titled *The Great Outlaws*. He stated that they were searching for a "Candy-like" figure, and if they found the right person, "who knows?" In 2017, there was also brief talk of Kevin Hart trying to reboot the film with Universal Pictures.

Although *The Great Outdoors* didn't achieve the critical or commercial success Hughes had hoped for, it has gained a cult following over the years and is now considered a classic.

12

Uncle Buck

Every artist has their muse, and from 1983 to 1986, Molly Ringwald was John Hughes'. However, after collaborating with John Candy on the success of *Planes, Trains and Automobiles*, Hughes would find in him both a close friend and a new muse. Unlike the 15-year-old Ringwald, Candy was someone Hughes could connect with on an adult level—a relationship the reclusive Hughes wasn't accustomed to. While Hughes often bonded with the crew on his sets, he was generally reserved, especially since most of his cast members were teenagers. But with Candy, Hughes found someone he could truly relate to.

They shared many common interests, including a love of hockey (even if their teams were rivals), and they both married their high school sweethearts, valued their families, and had two young children. In a March 2010 *Vanity Fair* article, Candy's daughter Jennifer said, "Our families basically merged." Despite living in different countries—Hughes in Chicago and Candy in Ontario—they regularly spent time together whenever they weren't filming.

After *The Great Outdoors* was released to modest reception in June 1988, Hughes, who was always writing, took a brief break. For Hughes, a break meant focusing on a single project rather than juggling multiple ones, as he had done from 1985 to 1988.

Hughes was now working on a project under his new deal with Universal. On October 7, 1988, he submitted the first draft of the film *Uncle Buck*. The film tells the story of a slovenly bachelor who is called upon to babysit his brother's three children during a family crisis. Despite his rough-around-the-edges persona, including being a freewheeling gambler with possible mob connections, Uncle Buck, like all of Hughes' characters written for Candy, has a good heart.

The success of *Planes, Trains and Automobiles* marked a turning point not only for John Hughes but especially for John Candy. Until then, Candy was typically cast in broadly comic supporting roles, as in *Stripes* and *Splash*, or as the lead in light, slapstick-driven films like *Summer Rental* and *Armed and Dangerous*. But *Planes, Trains and Automobiles* showcased a deeper, more nuanced side of his talent, prompting Hollywood to see him as far more than a lovable clown. Demand for Candy soared, and by 1988 he found himself juggling five different projects. His packed schedule became so intense that, despite Hughes writing the character of Buck Russell specifically for him, there was a real possibility that Candy wouldn't be available to play the role.

Universal was initially keen on casting Danny DeVito, especially after the success of *Twins* with Arnold Schwarzenegger, which grossed $216 million. However, DeVito turned down the role to direct and star in *The War of the Roses* alongside Michael Douglas and Kathleen Turner. Robin Williams and Jack Nicholson were also considered for the role. Ultimately, it was Candy's friendship with Hughes that brought him back to work with his buddy again, and he signed on to play the title role in *Uncle Buck*.

Even John Hughes recognized that his beloved Chicago might have been overused by this point, so he initially decided to set *Uncle Buck* in St. Louis for a change of scenery. However, when the winter of 1988-89 in St. Louis turned out to be unseasonably warm, the production relocated back to Chicago to capture the winter atmosphere as written in the script. Although St. Louis and Chicago are only about four and a half hours apart, St. Louis averages around 15.5 inches of snow per year, while Chicago, thanks to its proximity to Lake Michigan, averages 35.1 inches—a significant and reliable difference.

Filming began on January 4, 1989, at another abandoned school in Illinois. Just as Hughes had filmed *The Breakfast Club* at Maine North High School in Des Plaines, he chose New Trier High School in Northfield, Illinois, for *Uncle Buck*. Three of the school's gyms were converted into sound stages, where the interior of the Russell House and other key sets were built. The school also provided classrooms for the young actors and space for all the departments a film crew would need, including wardrobe, editing, a special effects shop, and a projection booth.

Although Hughes initially wanted Winona Ryder for the role of Buck's niece, Tia, he ultimately cast an unknown actress. The two younger children were also played by relative unknowns at the time— Gaby Hoffman and Macaulay Culkin. The following year, Culkin would become a bigger star than anyone in *Uncle Buck*.

In the now-legendary scene where Culkin's character interrogates Candy's character with rapid-fire questions, Candy generously stood behind the camera during Culkin's close-ups, even wearing handwritten lines from the script on his head to help Culkin relax and deliver his lines as quickly as possible. On set, Candy was known for his kindness, often inviting his fellow actors to dinner or offering them rides. According to a June 2016 *Vanity Fair* article, Amy Madigan, who played Candy's girlfriend Chanice, described him as an incredibly generous person and a true family man. Hughes believed that this warmth was part of what made the movie work so well, as Candy was great with the young cast, who adored him.

Filming for *Uncle Buck* wrapped on March 10, 1989. As with many of Hughes's later films, the initial edit ran about three hours long. This included many of Candy's ad-libs, as well as additional scenes that delved deeper into the relationship between Candy's and Culkin's characters, including how Buck helped his nephew make friends at school, a scene where Buck and his gambling buddies play Pictionary Junior and musical chairs for money, and a more detailed fight scene between Buck and the birthday clown. However, Hughes wisely trimmed the film down to a more appropriate comedy length of one hour and forty minutes.

The soundtrack for *Uncle Buck*, curated once again by music supervisor Tarquin Gotch, was notably different from any other Hughes film. It featured popular hip-hop artists of the era, like Young MC and Tone Loc, while also including English rock band Flesh for Lulu, who contributed two songs to the album.

John Candy was so beloved on set that he formed close bonds with many of the crew, including Gotch. One night, after a long day of filming, Candy offered Gotch a ride home in his limo. On the way, they spotted a bar Candy liked and decided to stop in. What started as a quick visit turned into an all-night party, as the two befriended other patrons and had a great time.

The next morning, a listener called into WLUP radio and excitedly shared, "You'll never guess who I was with all night—John Candy! We were at this bar, and he was in such great form that they kept the place open all night." Unfortunately, John Hughes happened to be listening to the radio at that moment and was furious upon hearing that Candy had been out all night before an important day of filming. Hughes immediately called Candy to express his anger and told him not to show up for work that day. Candy tried to explain that his character in that day's scene was supposed to look "disheveled," but Hughes was unmoved. He sent the cast and crew home, canceling the shoot for the day. Fortunately, the two made amends a few days later, which was unusual for Hughes after feeling disrespected.

Uncle Buck was released in theaters on August 16, 1989, meaning the entire process of shooting, editing, and releasing the film took just eight months. The critical reception was mixed, with few raves. Roger Ebert, in his review on the day of the film's release, noted, "The movie is filled with good intentions and good feelings, but they seem to conceal another side of Uncle Buck—a side that makes the movie feel creepy and subtly unwholesome." Ebert also speculated that Uncle Buck might have been inspired by the lovable, hapless character Candy played in *Planes, Trains and Automobiles*, suggesting that this could be a glimpse into the same man's life when he's not on the road.

Despite the lukewarm reviews, audiences were eager for more John Candy, and the film debuted at number one at the box office, though it faced little competition that weekend. *Uncle Buck* went on to gross over $66 million on a $15 million budget, ranking thirteenth at the box office for 1989.

When it came time to release the film on VHS for purchase or rental, the poster artwork was altered to better market it as a family-friendly movie. The original movie poster depicted John Candy knocking at the Russell family's door while the parents and three kids tried to block his entry. For the VHS release, the cover was changed—Tia, the older daughter, and the parents were airbrushed out, leaving only Macaulay Culkin and Gaby Hoffman blocking the door. This marketing strategy proved effective, as the film became an even bigger success in VHS rentals, ultimately grossing around $80 million.

The film's box office success, combined with Vincent Canby's *New York Times* review, inspired Universal Studios to consider turning *Uncle Buck* into a sitcom. Canby had remarked, "In *Uncle Buck*, John Hughes has had the good sitcom idea of placing Uncle Buck in the middle of an ideal suburb, in the middle of Mr. Hughes's idea of an average American family. The results are sometimes funny and, in the way of small-screen entertainment, so perfectly predictable that one could mail in the laughs."

Universal sold the television rights to *Uncle Buck* without informing John Hughes; he was furious. Hughes had been considering a sequel to the film, and the TV show not only spoiled any potential plans but also added insult by not involving him in the decision.

None of the original cast or crew from the movie participated in the short-lived series. It starred comedian Kevin Meaney and Audrey Meadows of *Honeymooners* fame. Created by Tim O'Donnell, the show's premise had Buck forced into babysitting again. However, to sustain the series, the plot took a darker turn—the parents were killed in a car accident, leaving Buck as the children's legal guardian. The pilot aired on September 10, 1990, on Monday night, but with low ratings, it was moved to Friday nights, where it struggled against the powerhouse TGIF lineup on ABC, including shows like *Full House*. Out of the 22 episodes taped, only 16 were aired before the series was canceled on March 9, 1991.

Hughes and Candy were outraged when CBS made the television series in 1990. This frustration resurfaced in 2016 when both the Hughes and Candy families were distraught to learn that ABC was planning another remake—once again without informing them. The families released the following statement through their attorneys:

> Disappointment has been expressed by both the John Hughes and John Candy families over the conduct and decision by the ABC Network and Universal Television to develop a comedy series based on the feature film *Uncle Buck*. Rather than either entity providing advance information to the Estates, the families learned of the project's potential via the media. The families feel a strong attachment to the original film, which symbolized the great and unique collaboration between Hughes and Candy. Recalling that the director was displeased with the first *Uncle Buck* TV show effort, which failed on CBS in 1990, it is well expected that he would not be supportive of this current attempt.

Despite the families' objections, ABC and Universal proceeded with the reboot, which they had every legal right to do. The new *Uncle Buck* series aired on ABC in June 2016, featuring an African-American cast, with comedian Mike Epps in the title role, and was filmed as a single-camera comedy. Like the 1990 version, this remake was poorly received by both critics and audiences and was canceled after just eight episodes.

13

National Lampoon's Christmas Vacation

After the success of 1983's *National Lampoon's Vacation*, Matty Simmons and Warner Brothers were eager for a sequel and repeatedly urged John Hughes to write it. However, Hughes, feeling the need to move forward with his own projects, declined. In 1985, Warner Brothers went ahead with *National Lampoon's European Vacation* without Hughes' involvement. Although the film wasn't well-reviewed and hasn't achieved classic status, it was a financial success, grossing over $50 million on a $17 million budget. In Hollywood, that kind of success usually means it's time for another sequel.

Matty Simmons, Hughes' former boss at *National Lampoon*, began pitching Warner Brothers the idea of a third *Vacation* film. It was Simmons who had originally suggested that Hughes expand his "Vacation '58" short story from the September 1979 issue of the magazine into a movie script, which became the original *Vacation*. Simmons also remembered that Hughes had written a sequel to "Vacation '58" titled "Christmas '59," which was published in the December 1980 issue of the magazine. After years of pushing, Warner Brothers finally agreed in 1988 to greenlight the Christmas-themed sequel.

Knowing Hughes's legendary aversion to studio interference, Simmons was unsure how Hughes would react to the news that Warner Brothers wanted him to expand on his "Christmas '59" story. To his surprise, Hughes was thrilled. He expressed his desire to produce the film and insisted on receiving first billing as a producer, with Matty Simmons serving as executive producer.

Warner Brothers agreed to the project with the condition that it be completed in time for Christmas 1989. This was a tall order, considering Hughes was already busy shooting *Uncle Buck* at the beginning of 1989. However, with *Uncle Buck* starting production in January 1989 and releasing in June of the same year, Hughes, known for his tireless work ethic, saw no reason why he couldn't film, edit, and release another movie by Christmas. After all, in 1988, he had three films come out in the same year.

Hughes had no intention of directing *Christmas Vacation* himself, so he sought someone he respected and wanted to help advance their career. He turned to Christopher Columbus, a Hollywood writer with credits but limited directing experience. Hughes sent Columbus the script for *Christmas Vacation* to direct.

At the time, Columbus had written the 1984 romantic drama *Reckless*, which didn't perform well at the box office. However, that same year, Steven Spielberg produced a script Columbus had written, which became the blockbuster hit *Gremlins*. Spielberg then had Columbus write *The Goonies* and *Young Sherlock Holmes* in 1985, both of which did extremely well at the box office. These successes led to Columbus's first directing opportunity with *Adventures in Babysitting*. Despite his writing achievements, industry expectations for Columbus's directorial career were low. In fact, in April 1988, the Chicago Tribune wrote of *Adventures in Babysitting*, "Chris Columbus, the writer responsible for such lame sub-Spielberg fantasies as *Goonies* and *Young Sherlock Holmes*, has been allowed to direct."

Adventures in Babysitting turned out to be a moderate hit, grossing $37 million on a $7 million budget. This success allowed Columbus to pursue a passion project for his next film, *Heartbreak Hotel*, a fictional story about the kidnapping of Elvis Presley. Unfortunately, the movie was both critically panned and a box office failure, grossing only $5 million on a $13 million budget.

At the time, both Hughes and Columbus were represented by the same agent, Jack Rapke. Hughes learned about Columbus's struggles and how he had moved to Chicago to escape Hollywood after the disappointing experience of *Heartbreak Hotel*. Hughes could relate, having gone through his own tough experience with *She's Having a Baby*. Recognizing Columbus's talent, particularly after seeing his work on *Gremlins*, Hughes thought Columbus might be a good fit for a darker kind of Christmas movie. He decided to send Columbus the script for *Christmas Vacation*.

Columbus, a huge Christmas enthusiast, had always dreamed of making a Christmas comedy. He was thrilled that Hughes thought of him for the project and was also in desperate need of a job, so he eagerly accepted the opportunity. The chance to work with a comedy legend like Chevy Chase was an added bonus.

The plan was set: Hughes and Matty Simmons would produce, and Chris Columbus would direct the third installment of the *Vacation* series. However, there was a known challenge—Chevy Chase. Though a big box-office draw at the time, Chase had a reputation for being notoriously difficult to work with. From his early days on *Saturday Night Live*, where he had a legendary backstage confrontation with Bill Murray, to more recent conflicts with directors and producers, including the infamous battles with Dan Harmon on the set of NBC's *Community*, Chase was not known for amicable on-set behavior.

In February 1989, Columbus had dinner with Chase to discuss the film before shooting began. The dinner did not go well. In a 2015 interview with *Chicago Magazine*, conducted by Hughes' son, James, Columbus recalled that "Chevy treated me like dirt." Despite desperately needing the work, Columbus found Chase's condescending and disrespectful attitude shocking, as he had never been treated that way by an actor he was supposed to direct.

Columbus, determined to keep the job and mindful that he was working under Hughes's watchful eye, initially stuck with the project. He began working on some establishing shots in February but decided to give his working relationship with Chase another try, hoping to smooth things over with a second meeting. Unfortunately, this meeting went even worse, and it became clear that Chase did not want to work with Columbus. Finally, Columbus called Hughes and told him, "There's no way I can do this movie. I know I need to work, but I can't do it with this guy."

Hughes completely understood. Having experienced Chase's difficult behavior during the filming of the first *Vacation* movie, he knew all too well the challenges that came with working with him. Hughes allowed Columbus to step away from *Christmas Vacation* and quickly began the search for another director, knowing the film still needed to be completed in nine months.

On August 27, 1987, legendary director Stanley Kubrick, known for classics like *2001: A Space Odyssey* and *The Shining*, gave an interview with Tim Cahill of *Rolling Stone* while promoting his new film, *Full Metal Jacket*. In a surprising revelation, Kubrick expressed his belief that some of the best art was now being created in TV commercials. As an American football fan living in London, he had been receiving videotapes of the week's games, complete with ads. Kubrick singled out a 1986 Michelob commercial, saying, "Michelob did a series, just impressions of people having a good time—the big city at night—and the editing, the photography, was some of the most brilliant work I've ever seen. Forget what they're doing—selling beer—and it's visual poetry. Incredible eight-frame cuts. And you realize that in thirty seconds they've created an impression of something rather complex."

Kubrick's praise prompted Hollywood to investigate which commercial he was referring to and who directed it. The ad in question was "The Night Belongs to Michelob," directed by Jeremiah Chechik. Shortly after, Chechik received a call from Steven Spielberg, who invited him to Amblin Entertainment to discuss potentially working on a small film for Warner Brothers, with whom Amblin had a distribution deal. Warner Brothers provided Chechik with an office as he prepared to direct a movie about the Apollo Theatre in Harlem. However, the studio decided to expand the project into a much larger film, a direction Chechik disagreed with, leading him to pass on the opportunity—a bold move for a young director, but one that did not diminish his standing at Warner Brothers.

Interestingly, the Michelob commercial that had garnered so much attention was created by Hughes's old advertising agency, Needham, Harper & Steers, which had since merged to become DDB Needham. With this connection, along with his status as a Spielberg protégé (like Chris Columbus), his reputation as a hot new talent at Warner Brothers, and the urgent need to replace Columbus on *Christmas Vacation*, Chechik was chosen as the director for *National Lampoon's Christmas Vacation*—his first feature film. Hughes, who had similarly taken a chance on Howard Deutch, saw no risk in the decision. On the first day of shooting, Hughes reportedly told Chechik, "It's your movie, man. You do it."

Principal photography for *Christmas Vacation* began on March 27, 1989, just seventeen days after the wrap of *Uncle Buck*.

Chechik got along very well with Chevy Chase, perhaps because, as a young director with no preconceived expectations, he was open to Chase's ideas. Ironically, Chechik did have several disputes with Beverly D'Angelo, who played Chase's wife in the movie.

Despite these challenges, the cast ultimately trusted John Hughes' writing. Producer Tom Jacobson noted that Hughes was a master of describing comedy in detail. Even scenes like the one where the squirrel jumps out of the Christmas tree were meticulously written by Hughes, ensuring the humor was perfectly conveyed.

                              CLARK
                    Shh! I hear it, too.

We hear a FAINT but distinctive, HIGH-PITCHED SQUEAL.

          ----

246 INT. LIVING ROOM

     The SQUEALING grows LOUDER. Everyone leans forward to
     listen closer.

     CLOSEUP—CLARK

     He leans down to the tree and has a listen.

                              CLARK
                    I don't hear it anymore.

     HIS POV

     Thick, fresh branches with charred ornaments and a
     single strand of lights.

     CLOSEUP - CLARK

     From inside the tree. Clark's hand separates the
     branches as he peers into the tree. A sudden look of
     shock.

     HIS POV

     A squirrel LEAPS INTO CAMERA.

     All hell breaks loose as a wild crazed, SHRIEKING
     SQUIRREL bursts into the room.

                              CLARK
                    Holy infant!

                              RUSTY
                    Squirrel!

     People are running every which way, bumping into each
     other. Nora faints dead away in the middle of the
     room. Lewis' cigar ashes spray as he rams Clark Sr.,
     Ruby Sue and Rocky are screaming at the top of their
     voices. The women are screaming. Art decks Francis
     on his way out. The squirrel goes up the drapes and
     leaps onto the couch.

Throughout the production of *Christmas Vacation*, Hughes maintained control over key decisions, particularly when it came to disputes with the studio about certain scenes. He had the final say on whether a scene stayed or went, and he consistently protected his young director, Chechik, from studio interference.

Filming for *Christmas Vacation* wrapped on June 30, 1989. After completing the first cut, Chechik arranged a private screening for Hughes. According to Chechik, Hughes praised the film, saying, "You've got such a great movie here, I don't want to tell you anything," a testament to his satisfaction with the final product.

The movie was released on December 1, 1989, to mixed critical reviews. However, the film delivered exactly what it set out to be—a slapstick Christmas comedy—which resonated with audiences. *Christmas Vacation* opened at number one at the box office, earning over $14 million in its first weekend and outperforming *Back to the Future Part II* in its third week. The film ultimately grossed over $53 million, ranking twentieth for the year in 1989, seven spots lower than *Uncle Buck*. However, with subsequent VHS and DVD releases, *Christmas Vacation* has earned over $71 million, becoming the highest-grossing film in the *Vacation* franchise. Despite being produced for different studios, Hughes Entertainment made over $137 million in 1989 alone.

Curiously, *Christmas Vacation* is a holiday movie that never actually shows Christmas Day—a quirk reminiscent of the original *Vacation*, whose initial cut ended with the Griswolds never reaching Walley World. In that case, Harold Ramis revised the ending after test audiences reacted poorly, ensuring the family finally arrived at their destination. But with *Christmas Vacation*, viewers didn't seem to mind the absence of Christmas morning; instead, they embraced the film wholeheartedly, and it has since become a beloved holiday classic.

Another unusual aspect of *Christmas Vacation* is that, unlike most Hughes films up to that point, it didn't have an official soundtrack. While bootleg versions have circulated over the years, no official soundtrack was ever released.

In 2003, Matty Simmons struck a deal with NBC to produce *National Lampoon's Christmas Vacation 2: Cousin Eddie's Island Adventure*, with Randy Quaid reprising his role as Cousin Eddie. The movie aired on December 20, 2003, attracting about 7.5 million viewers, earning a 4.6 rating, and winning its time slot that evening.

14

Career Opportunities

Even though Warner Brothers owned the rights to the *Vacation* franchise, Hughes still had his deal with Universal, and after the success of *Uncle Buck*, Universal was eager to produce another Hughes movie.

Since Hughes wasn't directing *Christmas Vacation*, he had time to focus on his writing after *Uncle Buck* was released in June 1989. During this period, Hughes developed a story about a 21-year-old man who gets locked inside a Target store overnight, where he meets a girl who had fallen asleep while attempting to rob the store to spite her father. The two spend the night together in the Target, falling in love, until their evening is interrupted by two unexpected robbers. This film, titled *Career Opportunities*, starred Frank Whaley and Jennifer Connelly.

In September 1989, Hughes delivered the script for *Career Opportunities* to Universal. Although he intended to produce rather than direct, he followed a familiar pattern and sought out a promising first-time filmmaker to helm the project. His choice was Bryan Gordon, who had recently won the 1987 Academy Award for Best Live Action Short. Hughes was struck by the strength of Gordon's short film—its sharp script and distinctive visual style—and decided he was the right person to bring the story to the screen.

With a director secured, Hughes, Gordon, and producer Hunt Lowry launched a nationwide search for the right filming location, ultimately choosing a newly renovated Target in Monroe, Georgia, just outside Atlanta. To accommodate certain sequences, the crew constructed additional department-store sets inside the building—a technique

Hughes's teams had mastered while building sets in abandoned Illinois schools on earlier projects.

Filming began on November 13, 1989, and continued through the holiday season. Because production overlapped with the store's busiest time of year, the crew worked overnight while the store was closed, occasionally enlisting employees who stayed after their shifts to appear as background actors.

Once filming began, Hughes took a hands-off approach, allowing Gordon to make "his movie" while remaining available if needed. At the time, Hughes was juggling multiple other projects. He reportedly visited the set only once, when his friend John Candy, as a favor to Hughes, made an uncredited cameo as the Target manager who hires Whaley's character Jim.

Without Hughes's constant presence on set, Gordon and the actors had the freedom to explore and develop character and narrative elements on their own. As Whaley noted in a March 2021 interview with *Yahoo Entertainment*, "With due respect to John Hughes, the script was a little thing. There was a lot of, 'Jim runs around the store, going nuts.'" Nonetheless, Hughes made it clear that he had the final say on anything that would appear in the finished film. Filming of *Career Opportunities* was completed on January 12, 1990.

Even when Hughes submitted a script he wasn't entirely satisfied with, he couldn't help but involve himself further, knowing his name would be attached to the project. After seeing Gordon's first edited cut of the film, Hughes became more involved, writing additional scenes and reworking the narrative to downplay the robbers and focus more on the romance between Whaley and Connelly's characters. Despite his efforts, Hughes was never happy with the finished product. In fact, he was so dissatisfied that he asked Universal to remove his name from the film and never release it. It's highly likely that *Career Opportunities* would have remained shelved, had it not been for events that transpired eleven months later.

15

Home Alone

In a December 2015 *Chicago Magazine* article, Hughes's son, James, revealed that on August 8, 1989, Hughes jotted down a movie idea in his notebook, inspired by what he called "traveler's anxiety." As Hughes explained to *Time* magazine in a December 10, 1990 article, "I was going away on vacation and making a list of everything I didn't want to forget. I thought, 'Well, I'd better not forget my kids.' Then I thought, 'What if I left my 10-year-old son at home? What would he do?'" Over the next nine days, Hughes completed the first draft of what would become the Christmas movie masterpiece, *Home Alone*. Despite his incredible productivity, Hughes, a notorious workaholic, even expressed concerns in the margins of his journal about working too slowly.

After finishing *The Breakfast Club*, Hughes contemplated expanding on Judd Nelson's character, John Bender. He wondered what life would be like for a social outcast like Bender if he stayed together with Molly Ringwald's wealthy character, Claire. Drawing from his experiences with "military brats" he knew growing up—kids who moved to Chicago's North Shore and felt out of place—Hughes wrote a script titled *Reach the Rock*. The story focused on a Bender-like character who spends a night in jail, conversing with the police chief in a battle of wits much like Bender and the principal in *The Breakfast Club*. This script had been lying around for some time, waiting for the right moment.

A year previous when Chris Columbus was offered the chance to direct Warner Brothers' big Christmas movie for that year, *National Lampoon's Christmas Vacation*, his situation with Chevy Chase had become so toxic he had to quit the project. Leaving the project and disappointing Hughes, Columbus feared it might end his directing career. Hughes was known for holding grudges, but fortunately he did not in this case. Instead, he offered Columbus a second chance. Much as he had once done with Howard Deutch—initially offering him *Planes, Trains and Automobiles* before shifting him to *The Great Outdoors* when Steve Martin joined the cast—Hughes sent Columbus two scripts in August 1989 and told him to "choose one."

The scripts Hughes offered were *Home Alone* and *Reach the Rock*. Although neither was a passion project for Hughes, if there had been one he was more invested in, it was likely *Reach the Rock*. *Home Alone* was intended as a small film that Hughes was ready to pass off, much like he did with *Career Opportunities*. Columbus, being a fan of the Christmas season and having longed to make a big Christmas movie, chose *Home Alone*. Despite being a writer himself, Columbus didn't mind that his name wouldn't appear in the writing credits. He was simply grateful for the opportunity to work with Hughes and to direct the film.

With Columbus on board, Hughes approached Warner Brothers to get approval for *Home Alone*. Warner Brothers agreed to a $10 million budget for the film. In comparison, *Christmas Vacation* had been given a $25 million budget, largely because the first two *Vacation* films were proven box-office successes. Hughes had yet to make a movie for Warner Brothers, as the success of *Uncle Buck* was under Universal, and *Christmas Vacation* hadn't been released yet.

As John Hughes, Chris Columbus, and former music supervisor-turned-executive producer Tarquin Gotch began pre-production on *Home Alone*, they quickly realized they needed more funding to create the film they envisioned.

Hughes approached Warner Brothers studio head Bob Daly to explain the situation. Although he had initially agreed to make the film for under $10 million, he now requested an additional $4.5 million—a relatively modest increase compared to the budget for *Christmas Vacation*. Warner Brothers countered with an offer of just $3.5 million.

At the time—fall 1989—Warner Brothers was heavily invested in the upcoming production of *The Bonfire of the Vanities*, based on Tom Wolfe's best-selling novel. The studio viewed *Home Alone*, a story about a boy left alone at home fending off burglars, as a minor project. Their focus was on making *The Bonfire of the Vanities* their blockbuster hit for Christmas 1990, much like *Batman* had been for the previous year.

Although Hughes wasn't yet aware of the enormous potential *Home Alone* would have, he was frustrated by Warner Brothers' reluctance to fully fund the project. He understood their priorities, given the success of Wolfe's book, but he didn't appreciate being "nickel and dimed." In response, Hughes submitted a detailed memo outlining why $3.5 million wouldn't be enough and explaining that they needed exactly $4.7 million to make the movie, with no room for further cuts. However, Warner Brothers insisted on additional cost reductions, and Hughes explained that nothing more could be trimmed without compromising the film.

Realizing he was once again facing obstacles with the studio he was working with, Hughes decided it was time to make a change.

In January 1990, Hughes met with Tom Jacobson, who had been managing Hughes Entertainment during the production of *Uncle Buck* and *Christmas Vacation*. The success of those films had not gone unnoticed, and Jacobson was offered and accepted a new role as executive vice president of production at Twentieth Century Fox Film Corporation. Hughes explained his frustrations with Warner Brothers to Jacobson, who then arranged a meeting between Hughes' agent, Jack Rapke, and the chairman of 20th Century Fox at the time, Joe Roth.

Roth was enthusiastic about the *Home Alone* script and surprised that Warner Brothers was giving someone as prolific as Hughes such a hard time over a relatively small amount of money. He was eager to make the film and wanted a copy of the script. However, it would have been illegal for Hughes, his agent, or Columbus to directly provide Roth with the script since Hughes was still under contract with Warner Brothers. The script was instead secretly delivered and received by trusted individuals on both sides.

Once Roth read the script, his excitement grew, and he told Hughes' agent, "If you can get it out of there [Warner Bros.], I'll make it." For Roth, it was a no-brainer: the film wouldn't cost much, and Fox didn't have a Thanksgiving/Christmas movie lined up. All they had to do now was wait for Warner Brothers to officially pull the plug, as Fox wasn't legally supposed to be aware of the project at all.

Columbus and Hughes continued to work on Home Alone as if everything was proceeding smoothly with the studio, but Hughes had a backup plan in place, in case Warner Brothers refused to provide the additional financing needed. Only a few people on the crew were aware of this contingency.

As with Molly Ringwald and later John Candy, Hughes often wrote characters with specific actors in mind. This was true for Macaulay Culkin as well. During the filming of *Uncle Buck*, Hughes and Candy were highly impressed with Culkin, particularly in two scenes. The first was the now famous scene where Culkin and Candy exchange witty banter back and forth. The second, which solidified Culkin in Hughes' mind as the ideal choice for *Home Alone*, was the scene where Culkin's character sits in a chair guarding the front door, peering through the mail slot and imagining villains on the other side. This image aligned perfectly with what Hughes envisioned for *Home Alone*.

Columbus agreed that Culkin was a great fit for the role after seeing him in *Uncle Buck*, but he felt it was wise to audition other child actors just to be sure. As a director, Columbus had much riding on an eight-year-old carrying a major film, especially since he was coming off a major flop. While Hughes was already an established filmmaker, Columbus was still trying to prove himself. Hughes, as was his style with directors he trusted, encouraged Columbus to take his time and do what he needed to do.

Janet Hirshenson, the casting director for *Home Alone*, held auditions in New York, L.A., and Chicago. She quickly realized that the role required a child no older than eight, someone who could convincingly believe in Santa Claus. Columbus auditioned over 200 kids, but as Hughes had anticipated, once Culkin read for the part, it was clear he was the perfect choice.

For the roles of the bandits, Daniel Stern loved the script so much that he auditioned, felt he could have done better, and asked to audition again later that day, which he did. Unbeknownst to Stern, Columbus had already decided to hire him.

The role of Harry was initially discussed with Robert De Niro, but it was never formally offered to him. When De Niro's name came up, Joe Pesci was considered. Columbus thought Pesci, who had shown his comedic chops in films like *Easy Money* and *Lethal Weapon 2*, as well as his dramatic work in *Raging Bull*, would be a great fit.

The pairing of Stern and Pesci was a success. The actors enjoyed working together, having previously shared laughs on the set of the 1982 film *I'm Dancing as Fast as I Can*. Fox executive Joe Roth later commented that he loved their contrasting heights, likening them to the comic duo "Mutt & Jeff."

However, as the production plans evolved, leading to budget issues, Daniel Stern's shooting schedule extended from six to eight weeks.

Stern assumed this would come with a salary increase, but Warner Brothers remained stingy with their budget. Interestingly, Pesci, who would go on to win the Academy Award for Best Supporting Actor in *Goodfellas* that year, had no issue with the extended schedule without a pay raise. Frustrated, Stern quit the movie, and Columbus hired actor Daniel Roebuck as his replacement. Roebuck rehearsed with Pesci for four days, but Columbus quickly realized that the chemistry between Roebuck and Pesci didn't match what Pesci and Stern had. Columbus and Hughes asked Stern to return, and Stern, later admitting that he let his pride get in the way, agreed to rejoin the project, realizing it was a movie he truly wanted to be a part of.

Hughes had known Catherine O'Hara for years through her collaborations with John Candy on *SCTV*. Throughout the 1980s, O'Hara auditioned for various roles in Los Angeles, but she was selective about the parts she took. She famously turned down the role of Beverly D'Angelo's character in *National Lampoon's Vacation* because, as Candy put it, she didn't want to play "the wife." However, in 1988, she found the kind of role she was looking for—a wife with a twist—in *Beetlejuice*. In 1989, she again played a wife, opposite Pesci, in Alan Alda's *Betsy's Wedding*, which also starred Hughes alums Molly Ringwald and Ally Sheedy. When Hughes and Columbus invited O'Hara for a meeting, they were already familiar with her work and hired her on the spot without requiring an audition.

As with *Career Opportunities*, there was no specific role written for John Candy in *Home Alone*. Hughes simply wanted Candy to be part of the film in any capacity. By early 1990, Candy was incredibly busy with various projects, including a voiceover role in Disney's *The Rescuers Down Under*, his live-action/animated Saturday morning show *Camp Candy* on NBC, and his own radio show, *Radio Kandy*. Knowing that he could only secure Candy for one day of shooting, Hughes offered him points on the film as a favor. Candy declined, insisting on being paid the minimum $414 required by SAG for a day's work. At the time, no one anticipated the massive success *Home Alone* would become, so it seemed like an incredible favor for a friend. However, this decision later became a point of tension in Hughes and Candy's friendship, as Candy grew increasingly bitter about not taking a share of the film's profits.

Candy arrived on set for what turned into an almost 24-hour shoot, improvising most of his dialogue. The scene was filmed at Chicago's Meigs Field Airport, which stood in for Scranton Airport—not O'Hare

Airport, as is sometimes reported. Meigs Field had only one runway, making it a unique location for the shoot.

In the early 1980s, John Candy and Eugene Levy created the Shmenge Brothers characters on *SCTV*. Yosh and Stan Shmenge, two brothers from the fictional country of Leutonia, were portrayed as the biggest polka duo in their country. The characters were so popular that in 1985, Levy and Candy produced an HBO mockumentary titled *The Last Polka*, which featured their *SCTV* colleagues, including Rick Moranis and Catherine O'Hara. *The Last Polka* was a loose parody of *The Last Waltz*, with Candy playing the clarinet and Levy on accordion. The characters became beloved, and it's believed that Hughes had this in mind when he wrote the character of Gus Polinski, the Polka King of the Midwest, for Candy.

Below is the original screenplay and dialogue for Candy as Gus Polinski, written by Hughes:

```
                         GUS
                   Maybe I can help.

Kate turns. A curly haired man in his late thirties,
GUS POLINSKI, stands beside her. Gus is dressed in his
travelling clothes. A sky blue banlon shirt, sansabelt
slacks, plastic loafers and a red satin jacket with the
words "GUS POLINSKI AND THE KENOSHA KICKERS" emblazoned
across the back. He is holding an accordion case. Gus
extends his hand.

         ------------------------------

                         GUS

         You a polka fan?

                         KATE

         A little. . .

                         GUS

         Ever heard of the "I Don't Want Her You Can
         Take Her She Can't Stuff the Kielbasa Polka"?

                         KATE

         Sounds familiar. . .

                         GUS

         That's us. Sold six hundred and fifty-eight
         copies. In Sheboygan alone. That's a record
         for a polka band.
```

                    KATE

Congratulations.

                    GUS

Yeah. We were playing a 'Holly and Hops'
party at the Asbury Park V.F.W. last night.
We got a Christmas gig lined up tomorrow at
the Milwaukee Jaycees. . .But they cancelled
our flight. So I sent Stash, my clarinet
player, to "Avis". . . He's gonna rent us a
truck. We're gonna brave this treacherous
weather and drive to Wisconsin. Since Chi-
town's on the way. . .

                    (smiles)

I figured you might like to hop a ride with
us. . .

The red jackets were changed to yellow, the truck was rented from
Budget, and Candy ended up playing the clarinet instead of the
accordion, as he felt more comfortable faking the clarinet. Candy was
the only actor allowed to improvise throughout the film, and given his
long history of improvisation with Catherine O'Hara, Hughes and
Columbus fully supported it. According to O'Hara, Hughes would
start a scene, Candy would pick up on it, and she would simply go with
the flow. This collaborative approach allowed Candy to completely
make the character his own, as seen in the final cut of the film:

                    GUS

I couldn't help hearing you've got a little
bit of a dilemma there. We've gotta crisis
ourselves. . .

                    (laughs to himself awkwardly)

                    GUS

Allow me to introduce myself, Gus Polinski,
how are you?

                    (seeing Kate's blank look)

                    GUS

Polka king of the Midwest?

                    (another blank look)

                    GUS

The Kenosha Kickers?

              (his bandmates all wave)

                    GUS

No? That's ok, I thought you might have
recognized. . . Anyways, uh, I had a few
hits a few years ago. Uh, that's why, you
know. . ."Polka, Polka, Polka"?

                 (singing)

Polka, Polka, Polka. No? Uh, "Twin Lakes
Polka." "Yamahoozie Polka," AKA "Kiss Me
Polka." "Polka Twist"

                    KATE

These are songs?

                    GUS

Yeah. Yeah. We. . . some fairly big hits for
us. You know, in the early '70s you know?

                    KATE

Oh.

                    GUS

Yeah, we sold about 623 copies of that.

                    KATE

In Chicago?

                    GUS

No. Sheboygan. Very big in Sheboygan. They
loved it, you know?

                    KATE
I'm sorry did you say you could help me?

The scene in the van where John Candy's character talks about leaving
his kid in a funeral parlor all day was completely improvised by Candy
around four o'clock in the morning. The crew struggled to keep from
laughing as Candy continued to make up the story. Director Chris
Columbus later mentioned that they had so much improvised material
they couldn't use half of it because Catherine O'Hara was having too
much fun with the guys in the truck when she was supposed to be
looking distraught over her missing child.

With the cast in place, production moved forward, and filming for *Home Alone* was to begin on Wednesday, February 14, 1990. However, three weeks earlier, on Friday, January 26, 1990, Warner Brothers unexpectedly pulled the plug on the production.

At the time, Warner Brothers had recently merged with Time, Inc., and the combined company needed to pay off $9.2 billion in bank debt by March 1993 across all its divisions, including television, movies, cable, and magazines. The studio was heavily focused on *The Bonfire of the Vanities* and was hesitant to invest more money in a film with an eight-year-old lead.

Warner Brothers placed *Home Alone* in "turnaround," a process where a film is put on hold, and the screenplay rights can be acquired by another studio. Some refer to this as "development hell." Associate producer Mark Radcliffe told the crew to go home that Friday and asked Hughes if they were officially laying everyone off. Hughes, however, told him to hold tight. As promised, Joe Roth at 20th Century Fox purchased the rights from Warner Brothers, and *Home Alone* moved forward under Fox. The film acquired the additional money they required and production resumed on Tuesday, January 30, 1990. Most of the cast and crew were unaware that their jobs had been in jeopardy, and when they returned to the set that Tuesday, they found "Fox" T-shirts waiting for them. Two weeks later, they moved production to Chicago and began filming on Valentine's Day, 1990.

The ending scene, where Kevin is reunited with his family, was shot on the second day of filming (February 15, 1990) because, like many Hughes productions, the team was chasing snow. They got lucky when a snowstorm hit Chicago that day, though they still had to use potato flakes blown into a fan to enhance the snowfall effect. After that, snow machines became a regular fixture on set.

Hughes once again utilized the abandoned New Trier High School for many of the interior scenes, though several key scenes were filmed at the actual house where the fictional McCallister family lived, located in Winnetka, Illinois. Columbus personally scouted for a house that was visually appealing, warm, and slightly menacing—one that would work for the film's stunts. He took photos of the exterior for Hughes' approval, and Hughes immediately recognized it as the perfect house described in the script. According to a 2015 *Chicago Sun-Times* article by Richard Roeper, the next Christmas Eve and Christmas Day in 1991 after the release of the movie, over 400 vehicles lined up outside the house. The family that lived there, the Abendshiens, often crammed into a bedroom with a hot plate while filming took place. The Abendshiens stayed in the house until 2011.

The film within the film, "Angels with Filthy Souls," supposedly released on November 26, 1938, isn't an actual movie, but the line "Keep the change, you filthy animal!" has become one of the most iconic in motion picture history. The fake movie was so convincing that many believed it was real. On December 26, 2018, Seth Rogen tweeted, "My entire childhood, I thought the old-timey movie that Kevin watches in *Home Alone*…was actually an old movie." Macaulay Culkin replied twelve hours later, saying, "Me too!"

"Angels with Filthy Souls" was filmed on February 13, 1990, just one day before principal photography for *Home Alone* began. When John Hughes sent the script pages, he simply titled them "the gangster film." The entire sequence was shot in a single day. *Home Alone* cinematographer Julio Macat was responsible for giving the short film its 1930s look and feel, meant to be a playful homage to the real 1938 Jimmy Cagney film, *Angels with Dirty Faces*.

According to a December 12, 2015, article in *Variety*, Ralph Foody, who played Johnny, was originally cast to play the role of Snakes, a part eventually played by Michael Guido. However, Foody had recently undergone knee replacement surgery and was unable to perform the physical demands of Snakes's dramatic death scene. As a result, director Chris Columbus decided to switch their roles.

In the original script ending, Marv and Harry were meant to be in prison, watching Angels with Filthy Souls" with fellow inmates. It was during this scene that they realized they had been duped by Kevin's trickery.

```
CLOSE-UP TV

The gangster movie's showing.

                MOBSTER

    Too bad Acey ain't in charge no more.

                  MAN

    What do you mean?

                MOBSTER

    He's upstairs taking a bath. He'll call you
    when he gets out.
```

```
                  MOBSTER
      I'll tell you what I'm gonna give you,
      Snakes. I'm gonna give you. . .

  493A INT. LOCK-UP-HARRY AND MARV-DAY

      They're in the day room watching TV with the rest
      of the offenders. They're dressed in blues. They
      look at each other.

  END
```

Hughes didn't mind when Columbus made minor script revisions because he trusted him as a fellow writer. One of the most significant additions Columbus made was the final scene of the movie—a scene so pivotal that it might be the reason *Home Alone* became an emotional Christmas classic. In Hughes' initial script, the character of Old Man Marley, the mysterious next-door neighbor rumored to be the "South Bend Shovel Slayer," saves Kevin's life by smashing Harry and Marv's faces with the shovel. He then winks and says, "A little trick I learned in South Bend," leaving open the possibility that he really was the "South Bend Slayer."

Columbus, however, added a deeper emotional layer to Marley's character. He introduced the scenes in the church where Marley confides in Kevin about missing his son, with whom he'd had a falling out, and a granddaughter he had never met. This led to the tear-jerker ending where Kevin sees Marley reunite with his son and granddaughter, having taken Kevin's advice to reach out.

In a 2020 interview with *Business Insider*, Columbus mentioned that this was probably his proudest contribution to the film. He suggested the idea, wrote a version of it, and two days later, Hughes sent back a rewrite that perfectly captured the emotional ending, something *Christmas Vacation* had lacked. During a 2020 interview on the *Today Show*, Columbus reflected on how the comedy and emotion still resonate, especially in the final scene, saying, "It just ties into the holiday season."

Filming wrapped on May 8, 1990, after eighty-three days.

Unlike previous films, where Hughes curated the soundtrack, he left the musical choices for *Home Alone* to Columbus. Columbus brought in his friend Bruce Broughton, who had composed the score for *Young Sherlock Holmes*, a film Columbus wrote for Steven Spielberg. In early 1990, Broughton was also working on Alan Alda's *Betsy's Wedding*, which, as mentioned earlier, featured Pesci, O'Hara, Ringwald, Ally Sheedy—actors with strong ties to Hughes. Broughton was also scoring *The Rescuers Down Under* for Disney, the same film John Candy was involved in, which was what limited Candy's availability to just one day on set.

While it wasn't unusual for composers to juggle multiple projects, Broughton informed Columbus, as the summer of 1990 approached, that he was under a tight deadline for *The Rescuers Down Under* and wouldn't be able to complete *Home Alone*. *The Rescuers Down Under* was released just one week before *Home Alone* in 1990. It's also rumored that the studio, Hughes, and Columbus weren't entirely satisfied with Broughton's work and joked about needing someone like John Williams to score their low-budget Christmas movie.

With the film's release only a few months away, *Home Alone* was still without a composer. In fact, some early posters even featured "music by Bruce Broughton" in the credits. Desperate, Columbus reached out to Steven Spielberg, who had produced *Young Sherlock Holmes* and *Gremlins*, both written by Columbus. Columbus asked Spielberg if he could connect him with John Williams' agent, which he did. Williams agreed to screen the film and see if he was interested. Again, unlike Simple Minds, who turned down work on *The Breakfast Club* after seeing it, Williams was enthusiastic about scoring *Home Alone*.

Williams created an original score that perfectly captured the holiday spirit while conveying a deeper meaning of Christmas. He incorporated the celeste—an instrument long associated with Christmas thanks to its prominent use in Tchaikovsky's "Dance of the Sugar Plum Fairy" from *The Nutcracker*. Its shimmering sound anchors the film's signature theme, "Somewhere in My Memory," which threads throughout the score. Williams' score was the final touch that softened the impact of the film's more violent scenes. As Columbus noted in a November 6, 2015, interview with *Entertainment Weekly*, Williams' score "took the movie to a whole new level."

When the movie was screened for the first time, Columbus described the atmosphere as being like a rock concert. Both Hughes and Columbus realized they had something special. Word quickly spread, and Joe Roth even heard from George Lucas that they had a hit on their hands.

Fox had been struggling since the departure of Alan Ladd, Jr. in 1979. Ladd, who had championed *Star Wars* as a viable project for Fox, left a legacy that the studio struggled to replicate under subsequent leadership. However, thanks to John Hughes and a story about an 8-year-old boy left home alone by his parents, Fox found its golden ticket.

In a February 24, 1991, *L.A. Times* interview, Roger Birnbaum, then president of Fox's worldwide production, remarked, "I felt like I was wearing a Super Bowl ring or holding up the Stanley Cup. We are no longer Sisyphus pushing the rock up the hill and having it come down on us. *Home Alone* is our golden cushion. It's made us solvent, taken the pressure off."

Home Alone was initially scheduled to open on November 21, 1990, the Wednesday before Thanksgiving. However, Fox became concerned about competition from Disney's *Three Men and a Little Lady*, the sequel to *Three Men and a Baby*, which had been the highest-grossing film of 1987. In turn, Fox moved the release date of *Home Alone* up by one week to November 16, 1990, believing it had a better chance of competing against *Rocky V* instead. Although this was still a gamble, given that *Rocky IV* had grossed over $300 million in 1985, Fox felt it was the safer bet.

When *Home Alone* opened on November 16, 1990, it debuted at number one, earning $17 million in its first weekend—beating *Rocky V* by $3 million and *The Rescuers Down Under* by $13 million. In its first full week, *Home Alone* grossed $27.3 million, outperforming the opening week grosses of both *Pretty Woman* ($15.9 million) and *Ghost* ($19.8 million), two of the biggest films of 1990.

While *Ghost* ended up being the highest-grossing movie of 1990, having been released in July, and *Pretty Woman* came in second after its March release, *Home Alone* quickly climbed the ranks. By the end of the year, *Home Alone* had earned $143 million in just a month and a half. When the dust settled, *Home Alone* had grossed $285 million, making it technically the number one movie of 1990, although it was closely followed by *Ghost*. In contrast, *Three Men and a Little Lady* ranked eighteenth for the year, and *Rocky V* came in at thirty-first.

Home Alone remained number one at the box office for twelve consecutive weeks, until February 3, 1991. It stayed in the top ten until June of 1991. By that time, *Home Alone* had become the third highest-grossing film of all time, behind only *Star Wars* and *E.T.* After its release on VHS, the film's worldwide gross neared $500 million.

Remarkably, *Home Alone* achieved this success without playing in the maximum number of theaters that a major release typically would. Columbus noted, "The feeling of seeing the film at number one at the box office week after week was remarkable. We just couldn't believe it, and part of that is the fact we weren't playing in 3,000 theaters; we were probably playing in 900, so the film was sold out a lot, and you got to see a comedy with a packed audience—there's no better way to see a comedy."

Despite its box office success, *Home Alone* received mixed critical reviews. *Entertainment Weekly* gave it a "D" grade, and Roger Ebert of the *Chicago Sun-Times* gave it two and a half out of four stars. On their show *Siskel & Ebert, At the Movies*, both Siskel and Ebert found the film childish and unbelievable. However, in February 1991, they revisited the film and nearly issued an apology for their initial review.

When Joe Roth at 20th Century Fox initially greenlit the movie and mocked Warner Brothers for hesitating over a $1.5 million budget increase, he considered himself lucky if the film made $40 million, viewing it as a "second-tier" project. Roth also acquired *Edward Scissorhands* from Warner Brothers that same year, a film that, on a $20 million budget, grossed $86 million.

On Christmas Day 1990, *The New York Times* published an article detailing Warner Brothers' disappointment during what should have been a festive season. The article noted, "After months of publicity and promotion, Warner had counted on something quite different for its latest offering. *Bonfire of the Vanities* cost about $40 million to produce and more to promote, but it took in a paltry $3.1 million in its opening weekend. For a movie with such a budget, $10 million would be more like it." The piece continued, "As if that were not enough to kill the Christmas spirit at Warner, *The Rookie*, the studio's newest Clint Eastwood action film, has taken in only about $14 million at the box office in the last three weeks. Also, the studio decided to pass on *Home Alone* when it felt the projected budget had grown too large. The film was made instead by 20th Century Fox, and it has been the season's big hit so far." This was written just one month after *Home Alone*'s release.

In the end, *The Bonfire of the Vanities*, Warner Brothers' pride and joy of 1990, ranked 131st at the box office and is now remembered as one of the biggest bombs in motion picture history. Meanwhile, *Home Alone* became not just a Christmas classic but one of the greatest family movies of all time.

For the first time in his career, a John Hughes film received Oscar nominations. Although the nominations were for Best Score and Best Song, it was still recognition at the highest level. In the end Williams would lose to John Barry and *Dances with Wolves*, along with Stephen Sondheim and *Dick Tracy*. However, *Home Alone* and Macaulay Culkin were also nominated at the Golden Globes for Best Picture and Best Actor. Though Pesci won Best Supporting Actor at the Oscars that year, it was for his role in *Goodfellas*, not *Home Alone*.

In just six years of filmmaking, John Hughes had run the gamut. He had pioneered a new niche with teen comedy-dramas, successfully branched out into adult comedies, and finally elevated the family movie genre, setting a blueprint for Hollywood in the years to come.

In early 1991, Roth and 20th Century Fox signed Hughes to a seven-film production deal worth $200 million. Hughes was now an even bigger Hollywood phenomenon than he had been after *Ferris Bueller's Day Off*.

16

Only the Lonely and *Dutch*

Columbus, like Hughes and many others who had the privilege of working with John Candy, became somewhat enamored with the actor. When Candy arrived to shoot his scenes for *Home Alone* in just one day, Columbus admitted he was nervous about meeting him. He had been a huge fan of Candy for years and worried that their interaction might go as poorly as his first encounter with Chevy Chase. However, the experience was the complete opposite.

After wrapping up *Home Alone* in May 1990, Columbus decided to write a small passion project screenplay specifically for Candy, titled *Only the Lonely*. The story revolves around a man in his late 30s trying to balance a relationship with a girlfriend and his controlling Irish mother. Many assumed that Columbus had created a remake of the 1955 Oscar-winning film *Marty*, which had won Best Picture, Best Director, Best Actor, and Best Screenplay for Paddy Chayefsky. However, Columbus clarified that while *Only the Lonely* was a nod to *Marty*, it was not a remake.

The last time Columbus had pursued a passion project after a hit film, *Adventures in Babysitting*, his follow-up, *Heartbreak Hotel*, had bombed, nearly ending his career. But this time, with the confidence that he and Hughes had a solid movie in *Home Alone*—though it had not yet become the phenomenon it soon would be—Columbus felt more secure.

Columbus sent the script to Hughes for feedback. Hughes thought it was brilliant and saw it as an intriguing vehicle for their friend, John Candy. Both Hughes and Columbus believed that *Only the Lonely* had the potential to showcase Candy's dramatic acting abilities, proving he was much more than just a comic actor. According to a 1991 interview with Candy, Hughes sent him the script, which Candy quickly read and loved. After a phone conference with Hughes and Columbus, they all agreed to make the film, with Candy starring, Columbus writing and directing, and Hughes producing. It would be one of the few films Hughes produced without writing, reflecting his confidence in Columbus after seeing a rough cut of *Home Alone*, unlike his experience with first-time director Bryan Gordon on *Career Opportunities*.

Only the Lonely also featured Hughes's alum Ally Sheedy as Candy's love interest and included a cameo by *Uncle Buck* co-star Macaulay Culkin. Interestingly, Hughes continued to work with Ally Sheedy despite having distanced himself from the rest of the cast from his earlier films, whom he felt had wronged him in some way. The film also starred Jim Belushi, who would collaborate with Hughes again in the future, and screen legend Maureen O'Hara, for whom the role of the controlling mother was written. Columbus had not initially realized that O'Hara had retired from acting, but she came out of retirement after meeting with Candy.

Filming for *Only the Lonely* began on October 1, 1990, just as *Home Alone* was nearing its release date. This allowed Columbus to focus on his new project while Hughes managed the numerous productions he was either writing or producing simultaneously. During filming, Jim Belushi noticed that Maureen O'Hara had a much smaller trailer than John Candy. Due to the film's tight budget, they couldn't provide O'Hara with a larger trailer, so Candy, out of respect for the screen legend who had worked with icons like John Wayne, swapped trailers with her.

As was typical for Hughes's productions, the film was shot in and around the Chicago area, with Candy playing a Chicago cop. Production wrapped on December 21, 1990.

In July 1990, John Hughes showed no signs of slowing down, continuing his prolific pace of writing, producing, and directing. He had just completed a screenplay titled *Dutch*, which can be seen as a reimagining of *Planes, Trains and Automobiles*. This time, however, the story focuses on a man named Dutch, played by *Married with Children* star Ed O'Neill, who is dating a divorcee with a 13-year-old son. Dutch offers to pick up the boy from his private school in Atlanta and drive him to his mother's home in Chicago. As usual, Hughes initially wanted John Candy to be part of the film, but Candy felt the story was too similar to a blend of *Planes, Trains and Automobiles* and *Uncle Buck*.

After Candy declined the role, Hughes considered other actors like Tom Hanks, Jim Belushi, and Bill Murray before ultimately casting Ed O'Neill. At the time, O'Neill was immensely popular due to the success of *Married with Children*, which, along with *The Simpsons*, helped establish the Fox network as a legitimate fourth major network. *Married with Children* would continue for eleven seasons.

Although *Dutch* is not widely recognized today as a John Hughes film, Hughes had high hopes for it. He chose Peter Faiman to direct, a significant shift from selecting Bryan Gordon, who had only directed a short film prior to *Career Opportunities*. Faiman was fresh off the surprise mega-hit *Crocodile Dundee*, which had grossed $328 million on an $8 million budget. Additionally, Hughes hired Alan Silvestri to compose the score. At the time, Silvestri was one of the top composers in Hollywood, having recently worked on blockbuster hits like *Who Framed Roger Rabbit* and the *Back to the Future* trilogy.

During the summer of 1990, Hughes and Faiman took a road trip through Georgia, the Carolinas, Mississippi, and Tennessee to scout the route that the film's characters would take on their drive back to Chicago for Thanksgiving. Hughes particularly enjoyed working with Ed O'Neill and frequently called him to discuss future projects, even inviting him over to his house several times during filming. It seemed Hughes was eager to forge a strong working relationship with O'Neill, similar to the one he had with Candy, and was almost like a child seeking a new best friend after Candy turned down the project.

Dutch began principal photography on November 24, 1990, just a week before Thanksgiving—a somewhat unusual start date, but necessary due to O'Neill's tight television schedule. As production continued into the new year, filming took place on Saturdays, Sundays, and Tuesdays, when O'Neill was off from taping *Married with Children*.

During the shoot, *Home Alone* was becoming a cultural phenomenon, which added excitement to the set as the cast and crew realized they were working on Hughes's follow-up project. Filming for *Dutch* wrapped on February 26, 1991, and the movie was released on July 19, 1991, just two months after *Only the Lonely*.

17

Curly Sue

In 1990, while Hughes was busy producing and shooting *Home Alone*, *Only the Lonely*, and *Dutch*, he began to consider the idea of creating his own mini-studio based in Chicago. He even contemplated acquiring the abandoned New Trier West school facility as a permanent soundstage. Though he was still considered a part of Hollywood, the North Chicago suburbs were already being informally referred to as "John Hughes's back lot."

Film historian and critic Neal Gabler remarked on Hughes's remarkable output, stating, "Certainly since the end of the studio system, no one has been as prolific as John Hughes. And even back then, when writers were cranking out scripts, no one did what he has been able to do—write and direct this many films. He is essentially performing the function of a studio all by himself."

Since Hughes had taken a break from directing in 1990, he focused primarily on writing that year. As he explained in a *New York Times* article from August 4, 1991, "If I'm on a roll, and I finish a script at 3:00, I'll start another at 3:02. I'll stay with it as long as it takes." He described this intense focus as "being inside the script," where time seems to disappear as he writes. "That's when you write and you look at the clock and it's midnight, and then you look at the clock again and it's 5 A.M. and you've done 30 pages and you don't know where it came from," Hughes added.

During that prolific year, Hughes was inspired by his younger sisters and the dynamic they shared with their aunts. He became fascinated by the relationships between little girls and women, leading him to conceive a film centered on a young girl. Realizing he enjoyed writing for female characters, Hughes noted that there hadn't been many comedies featuring a little girl as the protagonist. As he shifted toward family-oriented movies, Hughes toyed with the idea of characters who aren't initially family but gradually become one—wondering if that transformation could occur in just one week. This concept became the foundation for *Curly Sue*, the final film Hughes would ever direct.

Curly Sue faced numerous challenges from the outset. Production was initially scheduled to begin on October 15, 1990, but was delayed until November 13, 1990, just three days before *Home Alone* opened in theaters. The delay may have been due to Jim Belushi's concurrent work on *Only the Lonely*.

During production, Hughes and Belushi frequently clashed over Hughes's directing techniques. At one point, tensions escalated to the extent that production was halted because Belushi refused to come to the set. It was surprising for anyone to challenge Hughes at that time, especially since *Home Alone* was breaking box office records. Despite the conflicts, actress Kelly Lynch later reflected in an August 13, 2009, interview with *Entertainment Weekly*, "He made everyone who worked with him a better actor, there's no doubt about it. You felt like you had to step up for him."

Once again, the abandoned New Trier West school facility served as the set, and it became a magnet for Hollywood's biggest players. Industry insiders flew into the Chicago suburb, eager to collaborate with the man behind *Home Alone* and to witness his creative process firsthand. Every studio wanted a piece of the John Hughes magic.

The extended filming process for *Curly Sue* was largely due to John Hughes's meticulous approach, which co-star Kelly Lynch described as "burning more film than I've ever seen in my life."

Curly Sue was a project where Hughes faced several challenges in assembling his ideal cast and crew. John Candy was unavailable, Bill Murray turned down the role to shoot *What About Bob?*, and Alec Baldwin, who was originally cast, had to leave for a commitment on Broadway, a production of *A Streetcar Named Desire*. Ultimately, Hughes settled on Jim Belushi for the lead role. He had also envisioned Christina Ricci as Curly Sue after seeing her in the 1990 film *Mermaids*, but she was already committed to *The Addams Family*. Hughes even considered asking John Williams to compose the music after their successful collaboration on *Home Alone*, but Williams was occupied with *Hook and* Steven Spielberg, who always had his priority.

Filming for *Curly Sue* continued throughout the holiday season and wrapped up on March 23, 1991.

By this point, Hughes had grown increasingly disdainful of Hollywood executives. During the filming, Michael Eisner, then head of Disney, and Jeffrey Katzenberg, his top lieutenant, flew to the set after hearing about the success of *Home Alone*, hoping to secure a meeting with Hughes. However, Hughes intentionally kept them waiting, with his team repeatedly telling the executives that "Mr. Hughes is shooting an important scene now," or similar excuses. Eventually, Hughes allowed them to visit the set, a cold, damp alleyway filled with garbage, where they had to wait until he was ready. Hughes was clearly toying with them, making their visit as uncomfortable as possible. A Hughes Entertainment employee later revealed that Hughes enjoyed making things difficult for the executives, forcing them to sit in the alley with the rest of the crew amidst the rats and trash.

Despite his animosity toward Warner Brothers after their treatment of him over *Home Alone*, Hughes still made *Curly Sue* with the studio because they met his budget demands. However, he never truly forgave them. When he completed a rough cut of the film, he invited Warner Brothers executives to a screening but arrived an hour late. The executives, who had brought their wives and children, pressured the editor to start the movie without Hughes. The editor tried to delay as much as possible but eventually had to start the screening. When Hughes finally arrived and found the screening in progress, the editor was promptly fired.

18

1991

January
1990 was John Hughes's most ambitious year to date. While he had been highly productive from 1984 to 1989, directing and writing numerous films, 1990 marked an entirely new level of activity. Fresh off the enormous success of *National Lampoon's Christmas Vacation* in January, Hughes kept up a relentless pace until the summer, when he took a brief break—only to dive back into writing more screenplays. That year he produced five films and wrote four. Given the sheer volume of work, 1991 should have been a year for Hughes to bask in the rewards of his labor.

The unexpected and massive success of *Home Alone* captured Hollywood's attention. For two decades, it remained the highest-grossing comedy of all time. Hughes had managed to create a film that resonated with both children and parents, a validation of his unique ability to appeal to a wide audience. For someone known as a control freak, *Home Alone* was proof that Hughes could captivate teens, adults, and now children alike.

In a *New York Times* interview on August 4, 1991, Hughes reflected on the achievement:

One of the things I most enjoyed about *Home Alone* was that I made a segment of the marketplace laugh at things they don't usually laugh at. It wasn't just macho jokes. It was this little kid running around dropping paint cans on guys. And you could hear grown men laugh.

That was really satisfying to me. To be able to sit in a mixed audience, and they're all laughing at the same thing. That was really fun. I was sitting there saying to myself: 'I know how to do this.'

After *Home Alone*, Hughes became more sought-after than ever before. While he had already achieved significant success with films like *The Breakfast Club* and *Ferris Bueller's Day Off*, *Home Alone* propelled him to a new level of recognition. However, this heightened visibility also meant that his subsequent projects—many of which were already in the pipeline before *Home Alone* became a cultural phenomenon— would face unprecedented scrutiny.

At the start of 1991, Hughes was on top of the world, seemingly able to do no wrong. But the rest of the year would bring new challenges, revealing that even a master filmmaker like Hughes could encounter setbacks.

March

Unfortunately for Hughes, Universal Studios was still holding onto *Career Opportunities* and was eager to release another John Hughes film. After the debacle with the *Uncle Buck* TV series, Hughes had grown increasingly frustrated with Universal. Once again, the studio planned to release *Career Opportunities* without his approval, much like they did with the TV adaptation of *Uncle Buck*. Hughes proposed ways to fix the film, but the studio ignored his suggestions. He even attempted to buy back his name from the project, but after the massive success of *Home Alone*, Universal refused to let him do so. In a 1991 interview with *The New York Times*, Hughes remarked, "Now I'm a commodity. If *Home Alone* hadn't come out, my name wouldn't be on *Career Opportunities* four times." He had always feared disappointing people, and he felt that this film was a prime example.

Despite Hughes' objections, Universal released *Career Opportunities* on March 29, 1991, while *Home Alone* was still dominating the box office. To make matters worse, they marketed the film as a grown-up version of *Home Alone*, with the protagonist stuck in a department store facing off against two bumbling burglars. In Germany, the movie was even titled *Kevins Cousin allein im Supermarkt* (Kevin's Cousin Alone in the Supermarket).

Universal also tried to capitalize on Jennifer Connelly's beauty in their marketing efforts. Frank Whaley, who co-starred in the film, recalled seeing the movie poster for the first time on Sunset Boulevard and being shocked by what he saw. Producer Hunt Lowry admitted that the studio's goal was to create a poster that "popped." Lowry explained in an interview, "That poster, it became a star unto itself. It caught everyone's eye." Whaley quickly realized that no one was looking at him on the poster. The image featured Connelly in a revealing white tank top, which she wears in the film, but Whaley noted that he didn't recall her wearing that outfit during the poster photo session. It was later revealed that the studio had altered the image, cut-and-pasting a more plunging neckline into the final poster (this was done before the advent of modern photoshopping techniques).

Critics were merciless in their reviews. Roger Ebert summed up the general sentiment by calling the film "long at 80 minutes," but almost every review also mentioned, "Jennifer Connelly is very beautiful to look at." (The film's actual runtime is eighty-three minutes.)

Career Opportunities debuted at fourth place in box-office rankings, trailing behind three movies that had already been in theaters for weeks, including *The Silence of the Lambs* and *Dances with Wolves*. It finished ninetieth for the year, grossing just $11 million. Oddly enough, the film became a staple at Blockbuster Video, thanks largely to its iconic movie poster.

To add insult to injury, the soundtrack for the movie—briefly released on CD and cassette before quickly going out of print—was missing two of the most important songs from the film: "Nuthin On My Mind" by Soho, which plays during Connelly's solo dance scene in the music department, and "Where Are You Baby?" by Betty Boo, featured in the classic roller skating scene.

Despite its initial reception, *Career Opportunities* has gained cult status over the years, leading to a Blu-ray release in 2021.

May

On May 24, 1991, *Only the Lonely* was released. Since the film wasn't expected to be a blockbuster, there was little concern about opening it over Memorial Day weekend, even though it was anticipated to get lost in the shuffle. That weekend, *Only the Lonely* debuted in fifth place, trailing behind Bruce Willis' *Hudson Hawk*, Ron Howard's *Backdraft*, and *Thelma & Louise*—the latter two films eventually grossing a combined $200 million. For the year 1991, *Only the Lonely* ranked sixty-fourth at the box office with a total of $22 million, a modest figure for a film produced by John Hughes.

However, because this was the first Hughes/Columbus collaboration following the mega-hit *Home Alone*, audiences had high expectations. As a result, the movie didn't perform well at the box office and received mixed reviews. Despite its commercial performance, *Only the Lonely* holds significant importance in the Hughes canon for John Candy's performance.

Although the film didn't attract a large audience at the time of its release, Candy's portrayal was widely recognized as a breakthrough in his acting career. Hughes and Columbus were determined to showcase Candy's ability as a dramatic actor, and the film did just that. On May 24, 1991, *The Chicago Tribune* called Candy "indisputably charming." During a Tonight Show appearance on May 17, 1991, with both Candy and Maureen O'Hara, O'Hara praised Candy's acting so much that it made him blush.

When reviewed by Siskel and Ebert on their show *At the Movies* in May 1991, the critics were divided on the film itself but unanimously praised Candy. In their recap, Siskel criticized Columbus for not crafting a smarter script, while Ebert noted, "*Only the Lonely* is a movie that people may enjoy more than they expect to." Despite these positive remarks about Candy's performance, if people were keeping track of Hughes' post-*Home Alone* films, the tally now stood at 0-2.

July

Dutch premiered on July 19, 1991, but the scheduled premiere event was canceled because Hughes was already deep into his next project. Unfortunately, the reviews that followed its release did nothing to improve the situation.

The New York Times review on July 19, 1991, noted, "There's a John Candy-sized hole at the center of *Dutch*." The review went on to criticize Faiman's directing and the cast. *The Washington Post* was even harsher on the same day, stating:

When John Hughes puts his name on a movie, you can depend on at least two things: It will be just like those other John Hughes movies, and John Candy will be in it. In *Dutch*, screenwriter Hughes breaks one of his rules: Candy is noticeably missing. The other Hughes tradition, it seems, is sacrosanct.

The *Post* also took aim at Hughes's famously fast screenwriting process:

The enduring legend about Hughes is that he holes up for the weekend, loads up on junk food and good music, then cranks out a script by Monday. If that's true, then *Dutch* was finished, checked for typos, and on its way to Hughes's agent by mid-Friday evening. Hughes, a man more prolific than Stephen King, has produced yet another forgettable project. This movie shouldn't even be allowed on planes.

Dutch opened in tenth place at the box office, trailing $10 million behind that week's other release, *Bill & Ted's Bogus Journey*. It even fell behind *City Slickers*, which was already in its seventh week. The film ranked 142nd for the year and, for only the second time in Hughes' career, failed to recoup its budget. With a production budget similar to that of *Home Alone* at around $17 million, *Dutch* only grossed $4 million.

John Hughes had been Hollywood's golden boy for eight years, with only *She's Having a Baby* previously falling short of the public's high expectations for his work. Reflecting on the film, Ed O'Neill later remarked, "Any failure in Hughes' career, and he would bury it." O'Neill has openly expressed his dislike for the movie.

During the July 10, 1991, episode of *Late Night with David Letterman*, when asked by Letterman what it was like working with John Hughes, O'Neill, while promoting *Dutch*, replied, "If I was at a bar and I was in trouble, I wouldn't want to be with John Hughes because he'd be the first one out the back door." After the film's disappointing opening weekend, Hughes never spoke to Faiman or O'Neill again.

October

Curly Sue opened on October 25, 1991, with a modest start, placing second at the box office behind *House Party 2*. The film ultimately finished the year in fortieth place, earning $33 million on a budget of $25 million, marking another box-office disappointment for Hughes following the massive success of *Home Alone* just months earlier.

The reviews were overwhelmingly negative. Leonard Maltin criticized it as "a John Hughes formula movie where the formula doesn't work." *The Washington Post* was even harsher, with Rita Kempley writing in her October 25, 1991 review: "John Hughes serves up more of the usual mush in *Curly Sue*, a homeless poster-child movie that doesn't just tug at our heartstrings, it stretches them plumb out of commission. Hughes, who wrote, directed, and produced this altruistic marmalade..." Similarly, Owen Gleiberman from *Entertainment Weekly* commented on November 8, 1991: "One glance at this postpunk Shirley Temple and every kid in America must be thinking, 'It's the girl version of *Home Alone*!' How disappointed they will be."

At the beginning of 1991, Hughes was the most sought-after writer and producer in Hollywood. But by the year's end, he found himself relying on the success of a *Home Alone* sequel to restore his career—if he even still had the desire to continue.

19

Beethoven

By the end of 1991, critics were no longer as enchanted with John Hughes as they had been just a couple of years earlier. However, until mid-1991, Hughes was still the celebrated filmmaker who had brought the world *Home Alone*, and everyone in Hollywood wanted a piece of him.

In 1989, after leaving Universal in frustration over their unauthorized sale of the television rights to *Uncle Buck*, Hughes had to negotiate his way out of his contract. As part of the deal, he left behind a film and a script that Universal could use as they wished. One of these films was *Career Opportunities*, which Universal exploited by capitalizing on Hughes' newfound fame from *Home Alone*, despite his plea to remove his name from the project. The script he left behind was for a movie called *Beethoven*, a family film about a St. Bernard puppy who escapes a dognapping ring and finds refuge with a suburban family.

If *Home Alone* was the story of a boy defending his home from burglars and *Curly Sue* was about a girl taking on the world, *Beethoven* was the dog version of this formula. Hughes wasn't particularly pleased with the script, but as he often said, "If I finish a script at 3:00, I'll start another at 3:02." Unlike with *Career Opportunities*, Hughes insisted that his involvement in *Beethoven* remain anonymous, leading to the creation of his famous pseudonym, Edmond Dantès.

The pseudonym was inspired by Alexandre Dumas' character in *The Count of Monte Cristo*. In the novel, Edmond Dantès is falsely accused, imprisoned without trial, and forced to conceal his identity—a story that resonated with Hughes, who felt similarly about being tied to a script he didn't control. However, in reality there actually was an unidentified prisoner of state during the reign of King Louis XIV in France. His true identity remains a mystery even though it has been extensively debated by historians, books, articles, poems, plays and films.

In Hughes world, this was a fun joke for himself, family and friends. For Hughes, the pseudonym became an inside joke, a mystery within the industry—"Who is Edmond Dantès?"—a secret that, like Dumbledore's quote in *Harry Potter and the Sorcerer's Stone* (directed by Chris Columbus a decade after *Home Alone*) "What happened down in the dungeons between you and Professor Quirrell is a complete secret, so. . . naturally the whole school knows.," quickly became an "open secret" in Hollywood.

In 1991, Ivan Reitman, the producer behind hits like *National Lampoon's Animal House* and *Kindergarten Cop*, was approached by Universal to executive produce the secret Hughes script. Despite some recent misfires like *Stop! Or My Mom Will Shoot*, Reitman saw potential in the family-friendly *Beethoven*, especially after witnessing the success of *Home Alone*.

Reitman brought in writer-director Amy Holden Jones to rewrite Hughes's original screenplay. Jones, known for writing *Mystic Pizza*, which had received favorable reviews and launched Julia Roberts' career, described the project as "a huge rewrite of a script that the original writer had disowned." Jones ended up sharing screen credit with Hughes under the Edmond Dantès pseudonym.

Beethoven began filming on May 1, 1991, and wrapped on July 26, 1991. Despite Universal's concerns—including the decision not to market the film under Hughes' real name, the mid-production replacement of director Steve Rash with Brian Levant, and worries about the on-screen age difference between Charles Grodin and Bonnie Hunt—the film was released on April 3, 1992. It opened in third place behind *White Men Can't Jump* and *Basic Instinct*, both of which had already been in theaters for weeks. Nevertheless, *Beethoven* went on to gross $150 million on an $18 million budget, becoming a surprise hit, particularly overseas.

On May 17, 1992, after *Beethoven*'s success, the *New York Times* revealed that Edmond Dantès was, in fact, John Hughes. With the film's success, Universal quickly rushed a sequel into production, releasing *Beethoven's 2nd* the following year. The sequel, made on a smaller budget, grossed $118 million on a $15 million budget. This success led to a series of direct-to-DVD sequels in the early 2000s and further revivals in 2008, 2011, and 2014. In 1994, Ivan Reitman oversaw the creation of the *Beethoven* animated series on CBS. While Hughes may have distanced himself from the project, the legacy of Edmond Dantès and Amy Holden Jones lives on in every iteration of the franchise.

20

Home Alone 2: Lost in New York

In 1987, *Planes, Trains and Automobiles* marked a significant milestone in John Hughes' career as he successfully transitioned into adult comedy. Just three years later, Hughes would evolve again, this time focusing on family films. Principal photography for *Home Alone* began on Valentine's Day 1990, and exactly one year later, Hughes was once again the talk of Hollywood. On Valentine's Day 1991, after a competitive bidding war for his talents between Fox, Paramount, and Columbia, Hughes signed a $200-million, seven-film deal with Fox.

According to the *Los Angeles Times*, under this agreement, Hughes would produce, write, and in some cases, direct six films for Fox, each with a budget of roughly $20 million to $25 million over the next several years, totaling at least $120 million in production costs. Although the budgets were below industry averages, Hughes' fees were substantial. Fox would also provide funds for prints and advertising, which typically ran at least $10 million per film. Columbia had offered Hughes $18.5 million in fees for five films (excluding *Home Alone*) with minimal creative input from the studio, but Fox's deal included considerable creative control over the projects. The seventh film Hughes was required to make under this agreement was the sequel to *Home Alone*, the original having already grossed $176 million by February 14, 1991, on its way to nearly half a billion dollars worldwide.

Having never written a sequel before, Hughes spent the summer of 1991 drafting four different versions of *Home Alone 2*. The version he ultimately chose to develop and shoot for Fox was set in New York City. He also wrote a version titled "Lost in Milwaukee," which made more sense geographically, given the McCallister family's home base near Chicago. However, New York was deemed a more "sexy" setting, and so it was chosen. Hughes admitted that it was challenging not to simply rehash the first film.

In February 1989, following the unexpected success of 1985's original *Back to the Future*, Robert Zemeckis and Steven Spielberg decided to film *Back to the Future Part II* and *Part III* simultaneously and release them a year apart. A similar idea was considered for *Home Alone 2* and *Home Alone 3*, but it never came to fruition.

Originally titled *Alone Again*, the script for *Home Alone 2* found a way to revisit the same story while introducing new twists and clever nods to the first film. For example, the scene where the family loads the van for the airport, nearly forgetting Kevin again, only to have him pop up from behind the front seat, or the moment when the burglars anticipate paint cans, remembering their last encounter, only to be hit with a metal beam instead. These callbacks were crucial to Hughes and Columbus's goal of not disappointing the young audience who had loved the first film.

Columbus admitted in a 1992 interview that he was initially concerned about whether he and Hughes could recreate the magic and impact of the original film in a sequel. However, he expressed confidence that they had succeeded in the *Making of Home Alone 2* special, which aired on Fox television on November 1, 1992, three weeks before the movie's release. Columbus emphasized the importance of capturing the essence of New York in the film, making it appear both gritty and frightening at times, while also showcasing its beauty and excitement.

Hughes initially wrote a returning role for John Candy's character, Gus Polinski, in *Home Alone 2*, but Candy was still bitter about his compensation for the first *Home Alone* film. Columbus recalled that Candy would frequently express his frustration on the set of *Only the Lonely*, which was being filmed as *Home Alone* was becoming a massive hit. Unable to reach a financial agreement, Candy ultimately did not return for the sequel. Between Candy disappointing Hughes with *Dutch* and now *Home Alone 2*, this marked the beginning of a growing distance between Hughes and Candy, whose once-close friendship was starting to fray, a pattern that Hughes had experienced with others in his life.

Securing the original cast for the sequel was "vital," according to Hughes, with Macaulay Culkin being the most important piece. However, Culkin's father and manager, who was known for being difficult behind the scenes, threatened to pull Macaulay from the project unless Fox also cast him in the lead role of the horror movie *The Good Son*. Eventually, Culkin got the role in *The Good Son* and was paid $4.5 million plus five percent of the film's gross for *Home Alone 2*, a significant jump from the $110,000 he earned for the first *Home Alone*.

In March 1991, Joe Pesci had just won the Academy Award for Best Supporting Actor for *Goodfellas*. That same year, he was filming several major projects, including Oliver Stone's *JFK*, the hit franchise sequel *Lethal Weapon 3*, and the soon-to-be-discovered *My Cousin Vinny*. Getting Pesci back for *Home Alone 2* was also costly, with sources indicating he was paid between $2 and $3 million. Between Pesci and Culkin, the studio had already spent $8 million of the film's $28 million budget.

Principal photography for *Home Alone 2: Lost in New York* began on December 9, 1991, and wrapped on May 6, 1992. Ironically, after years of filming in Chicago and the Midwest, often searching for snow, *Home Alone 2* didn't need fake snow, as a blizzard hit New York City right before filming began.

Hughes regular Ally Sheedy, the only member of the "Brat Pack" still in contact with Hughes, had a cameo as a ticket agent. Chris Columbus also revealed that in order to use New York's Plaza Hotel, which was owned by Donald Trump at the time, Trump insisted on making a cameo appearance. Trump, at that time, was a "must have" cameo if you were filming in New York City.

Just before filming commenced, Hughes had a brilliant idea: he invented a fictional device called the "Talkboy." Knowing that Kevin, Culkin's character, would need to pass himself off as an adult at various points, especially in the New York City hotel, Hughes envisioned a futuristic recording device that could alter a person's voice. Although the original script mentioned Kevin's Walkman, Hughes changed it to the Talkboy.

Mattel was initially set to handle the marketing, licensing, and merchandising but negotiations fell through, and Tiger Electronics took over. Known primarily for their handheld gaming devices, Tiger worked with Hughes to develop the Talkboy exactly as he had imagined.

The silver hardshell device fit in the palm of a child's hand and came equipped with a slot-like handle on the back for an easy grip. It featured a telescoping microphone and a cassette tape for recording sounds and conversations. A tuner allowed those recorded snippets to be slowed down or sped up for playback, creating a groggy, low-pitched tone or a squeaky, chipmunk-like cadence, respectively.

Hughes, Tiger, and Fox were so pleased with the Talkboy that they decided to manufacture it for sale at $29.99, expecting it to be a hit. While initial sales were moderate, demand surged after the movie was released on VHS in July 1993, with the VHS box including a brochure for a new sound-effects Talkboy that fixed some of the earlier bugs. The device became the must-have toy of 1993, but Tiger was caught off guard by the incredible demand and struggled to keep up with production. Once again, Hughes had turned a small idea into a massive success.

John Williams returned to compose the score for *Home Alone 2*, and two separate soundtracks were released. One featured Williams' score, while the other included Christmas music featured in the film. This approach mirrored what Warner Brothers had done in 1989 with *Batman*, releasing one soundtrack with Danny Elfman's score and another with music by Prince.

Home Alone 2: Lost in New York premiered on November 20, 1992. The reviews were mixed, with many critics acknowledging that while the film was predictable and followed the same formula as the original, it still delivered holiday cheer and entertainment for its target audience—kids and families. Janet Maslin of *The New York Times* noted in her review on the release date, "*Home Alone 2* may be lazily conceived, but it is staged with a sense of occasion and a lot of holiday cheer. The return of Mr. Culkin (the one-boy box-office phenomenon) in this role is irresistible."

However, not all reviews were positive. Siskel and Ebert gave the film two thumbs down, citing the excessive violence as a significant issue. Kenneth Turan of the *Los Angeles Times* criticized the film in his November 20, 1992, review, stating, "Less a successor to the original *Home Alone* than a relentless attempt at exact duplication." Despite these critiques, the film's success at the box office was undeniable. Three days after its release, the *Los Angeles Times* ran the headline, "Holy Cow! *Home [Alone]* 2 Hauls in Box-Office Moola."

The film easily debuted at number one, grossing $31 million in its opening weekend. By the end of 1992, *Home Alone 2* had finished third in the year's box office rankings, behind two other sequels— *Batman Returns* and *Lethal Weapon 3*, the latter also featuring Joe Pesci. Ultimately, *Home Alone 2: Lost in New York* would earn over $359 million worldwide.

21

Dennis the Menace and *Baby's Day Out*

In 1992, John Hughes was discouraged by the lukewarm response to his more personal projects, yet he took comfort in his solid reputation as the leading creator of family comedies. He didn't know yet that *Home Alone 2* would become another box office smash, but he was confident it would perform well and was already thinking about the possibility of a *Home Alone 3*.

After the runaway success of the original *Home Alone*, Hollywood was eager to find the next Hughes-style hit. One property that seemed to fit the formula was the comic strip *Dennis the Menace*, centered on a mischievous child whose antics constantly upended the lives of the adults around him. The character had already enjoyed success in other media, including a popular live-action CBS series that ran from 1959 to 1963 and a Saturday-morning animated version that aired in the 1980s.

In 1991, Warner Brothers became interested in acquiring the rights to the property from its creator, Hank Ketcham, who was open to the idea of a film adaptation. Ketcham had been dissatisfied with the television show, believing that Jay North, the actor who played Dennis, was too old for the role. This sparked a bidding war for the rights, with 20th Century Fox (the studio behind *Home Alone*), Walt Disney, and Steven Spielberg's production company at Universal all vying for the project.

Ernest Chambers, the veteran television writer and producer behind *The Smothers Brothers Comedy Hour* and *The Merv Griffin Show*, was a longtime collaborator of Ketcham's. Under Ketcham's guidance,

Chambers had been developing a *Dennis the Menace* musical and had already completed the book for the show. Although the project managed a few performances in a Washington, D.C. suburb, it never secured consistent composers or lyricists and eventually fell apart.

Chambers's connections included colleagues who had previously written and produced the Broadway show *Pump Boys and Dinettes*. He was asked to produce a pilot for NBC for a possible series based on *Pump Boys*. One of the writers of the musical, John Schimmel, had become an executive at Warner Brothers by 1991. Since Hughes still had an existing contract with Warner Brothers, Chambers saw an opportunity to bring *Dennis the Menace* to Hughes' attention. Warner Brothers was also in the early stages of launching their Warner Brothers Family Entertainment production division, making *Dennis the Menace* a perfect fit for their first project. Hughes found the project intriguing and was hired as the writer-producer.

True to form, Hughes quickly wrote the script. However, according to the Academy of Motion Picture Arts and Sciences files, he spent 40 days in the spring of 1992 evaluating over 20,000 video submissions from five and six-year-old boys during a nationwide casting call.

Hughes ultimately chose a young director, Patrick Reed Johnson, to helm the project after being impressed by Johnson's 1990 film *Spaced Invaders*, a low-budget comedy science fiction film.

A year earlier, Hughes had handed Johnson the script for *Reach the Rock*, much like he had done with Chris Columbus. Johnson was thrilled at the prospect of directing Hughes's first serious film, but he quickly became overwhelmed at the thought of taking on such a project. According to Johnson, Hughes spent an entire night discussing the project with him in his office, saying, "You're good. I know you're good, and you're going to get even better. I'll help you get there. Come make this movie with me. You want to shoot a million feet of film? I'll protect you. You want this actor, that actor? I'll get them for you!"

Despite Hughes's encouragement, Johnson ultimately felt that he wasn't the right fit for the project and preferred working with special effects and tricks, so he passed on the opportunity, much like Columbus had done with *Christmas Vacation*.

A year later, when Hughes began looking for a director for *Dennis the Menace*, he decided to give Johnson another opportunity. Johnson helped cast the lead role and started prepping the film. (Mason Gamble, who was ultimately cast as Dennis, was the son of Tim Gamble, who appeared as Molly Ringwald's father in the opening scene of Hughes's

The Breakfast Club.) But as Johnson later recalled, "Each day I grew less and less fond of the script, so I started trying to shift the story in different directions." One of his proposed changes involved a major new introduction for the villain, played by Christopher Lloyd. Hughes listened and nodded, giving the impression he was open to the idea. The next day, however, Johnson was fired. When he asked his agent what had happened, the answer was blunt: "John says you're trying to change his script."

Hughes's next choice for director was Nick Castle. Castle had transitioned from working with legendary horror director John Carpenter—having played Michael Myers in the original *Halloween* and written *Escape from New York*—to writing family-friendly films like *The Last Starfighter* and Spielberg's *Hook*. This made him a fitting choice for *Dennis the Menace*.

Hughes originally wanted John Candy to play Mr. Wilson, but Candy declined. Though Hughes always hoped to collaborate with Candy, Walter Matthau was cast in the role, and Hughes was thrilled to work with the legendary actor.

Principal photography for *Dennis the Menace* began on August 3, 1992, and wrapped on January 12, 1993.

Dennis the Menace had a big premiere at Mann's Chinese Theater on June 19, 1993, as it was the first film from Warner Brothers' new Family Entertainment division. The film opened to the public on June 25, 1993. Critics were not impressed, with many drawing unflattering comparisons between Mason Gamble and Macaulay Culkin, and criticizing Christopher Lloyd's character, Switchblade Sam, as being too violent for a family film. Some even labeled it as "Home Alone 3," but Hughes shrugged off the comparisons, saying in a 1993 interview, "He's blonde and it's a comedy, I get it. But it's fundamentally different. Dennis has no clue what he's doing, and that's the difference."

The *Los Angeles Times* review by Peter Rainer on June 25, 1993, was skeptical, stating, "If Hughes was expecting this film to create another pipsqueak franchise for him, he may have miscalculated." However, the film proved the critics wrong by debuting at number three at the box office, just behind *Sleepless in Seattle* with Tom Hanks and Meg Ryan. It finished twentieth for the year, grossing over $117 million after its release on VHS, making it a bona fide hit.

Even before filming had wrapped, on September 10, 1992, *Daily Variety* reported that Walter Matthau had already signed on for a sequel. After filming concluded in early 1993, the *Los Angeles Daily*

News confirmed that Mason Gamble would reprise his role as Dennis. Hughes expressed interest in making a sequel and working with Matthau and Gamble again in a 1993 interview.

Although two sequels were made five years later—*Dennis the Menace Strikes Again* in 1998 and *A Dennis the Menace Christmas* in 2007—neither involved Hughes or the original cast. Both were released straight to video.

Before *Dennis the Menace* had even started principal photography, Hughes was writing his next film, which entered early development in June 1992. He had been steadily moving toward younger protagonists within his "Home Alone" formula: first an eight-year-old in *Home Alone*, then a six-year-old in *Dennis the Menace*, and now he planned to center a story around a nine-month-old baby. This new project would be part of his seven-picture deal with Fox.

Despite the box-office success of *Dennis the Menace*—and his public interest in making a sequel—Hughes remained deeply dissatisfied with the final film. His frustration ran so deep that he contacted the project's original director, Patrick Read Johnson, whom he had fired early in production. According to a 2001 interview with Johnson, Hughes opened their conversation by asking, "Do you hate me?" He then admitted he had made a mistake: "There were other people I should have fired, not you. But I'm going to make it up to you." Hughes followed that apology by offering Johnson his next film, *Baby's Day Out*.

Thanks to the success of *Home Alone*, *Home Alone 2*, and *Dennis the Menace*, Fox approved a substantial $50 million budget for *Baby's Day Out*, an unusually high amount for a film without major stars. Principal photography began on August 17, 1993, and wrapped on December 16, 1993.

During filming, Hughes would occasionally visit the set and review the dailies, offering suggestions but largely allowing Johnson to direct the film as written. Even though Johnson had some issues with the script, he chose to keep his concerns to himself this time.

However, things began to unravel during the editing process. After several disappointing test screenings of Johnson's initial cut, Hughes took it upon himself to re-edit the film and present his version to Fox executives on March 3, 1994. Unfortunately, this version also failed to impress.

Hughes and Johnson found themselves at odds over whose version of the film was better. Eventually, they decided to collaborate and went back to Hughes' house to watch the film together, aiming to identify what worked and what didn't. They resolved to return to the editing room the next day to make the necessary improvements.

But on March 4, 1994, John Candy passed away. Although Hughes and Candy had not spoken in a year or two, Candy's death deeply affected Hughes. In the wake of Candy's passing, Hughes lost his passion for *Baby's Day Out*. A few weeks later, he told Johnson, "Let's just cut the film and be done with it, and then we never have to see each other again."

Baby's Day Out was initially slated for release in September 1994, allowing ample time for further edits. However, when James Cameron's *True Lies* was delayed, Fox decided to move *Baby's Day Out* to the July 1 release slot, originally intended for *True Lies*. This move cut two crucial months from the film's post-production schedule.

Baby's Day Out opened on July 1, 1994, to mixed, though not terrible, reviews. Unfortunately, the decision to move the release date placed the film in direct competition with *The Lion King*, which dominated the weekend box office with $34 million. *Baby's Day Out* ranked ninth, earning just $4 million. Ultimately, the film was a major box office flop, grossing only $16 million against its $50 million budget and finishing eighty-sixth for the year.

Disillusioned with Hollywood, frustrated by the studios, and grieving the loss of his close friend John Candy, Hughes decided he had had enough. He retreated from the business, moved back to Chicago, and withdrew from public life.

22

The Death of John Candy

John Candy was universally beloved, both in everyday life and within the Hollywood circle. His warm personality and genuine kindness endeared him to all who knew him.

A famous anecdote from Super Bowl XXIII illustrates just how adored he was: with under four minutes left in the game, and the San Francisco 49ers trailing the Cincinnati Bengals by three points, quarterback Joe Montana famously pointed out Candy in the stands to his teammates before throwing the game-winning touchdown pass. This moment captured Candy's unique ability to bring a sense of calm and joy to any situation, even a high-pressure sporting event.

However, after his breakout role in *Splash* (1984), Candy's career hit a rough patch. A series of films, including *Brewster's Millions*, *Summer Rental*, *Volunteers*, and *Armed and Dangerous*, all underperformed at the box office. These setbacks deeply affected Candy, who was known to be a sensitive soul. The pressure of staying relevant in Hollywood weighed heavily on him, leading him to cope through overeating and smoking, habits that ultimately harmed his health.

In 1986, Candy received an untitled script from John Hughes, which he saw as a potential career-saving opportunity—and it was. The success of *Planes, Trains and Automobiles* (1987) not only solidified Candy as a leading star but also proved Hughes could handle more than just teenage comedies. Their collaboration became a mutual charm, with each boosting the other's success.

Candy's newfound stardom allowed him to choose his projects, but unfortunately, he often made poor decisions. Films like *Hot to Trot*,

Who's Harry Crumb?, *Cannonball Run 3*, *Nothing but Trouble*, and *Delirious* all flopped. Despite these missteps, Candy found success in Hughes-penned or -produced films like *Uncle Buck* and *Only the Lonely*, with his legendary cameo in *Home Alone* further cementing his status as a beloved actor.

The friendship between Candy and Hughes, though strong, was not without its strains. After a falling out during the filming of *Uncle Buck*, when Candy stayed out late and Hughes canceled the day's shoot in anger, the two managed to reconcile. However, Candy's decision to turn down a stake in *Home Alone*—a decision he would come to regret—caused tension between them. Candy had even planned to buy an apartment in Chicago, assuming his collaboration with Hughes would continue.

But by the early 1990s, Candy's career had taken another downturn, compounded by his refusal to star in Hughes's films *Dutch* and *Dennis the Menace* (though one was turned down for a role in Oliver Stone's *JFK*). This led to a cooling of their relationship, as Hughes, who took such rejections personally, began to distance himself from Candy.

By 1993, Candy was facing not only a string of film failures but also personal challenges. His involvement with the Toronto Argonauts, a Canadian Football League team he co-owned with hockey legend Wayne Gretzky, ended in disappointment. Candy loved being part of the team but struggled to give it the attention it required, leading to the unraveling of his ownership stake and adding to his growing list of woes.

Candy had hoped that his friend John Hughes might once again come to his aid and help revive his career. But Hughes, as he was known to do, stopped returning his calls. Tarquin Gotch, who had grown close to Candy, shared a similar experience of confusion over his friendship with Hughes. Gotch, who had been Hughes's go-to music supervisor and later an executive producer, found himself similarly cast out after *Home Alone*. Reflecting on their friendship, Gotch once remarked, "One day he would treat you as his best friend, and the next you would be exiled to Siberia, without a word of explanation." This sudden estrangement left Candy devastated.

Despite this setback, Candy managed to regroup. He fired his agency, ICM, and signed with CAA, who secured him a role in a promising Disney project, *Cool Runnings*. The film, made for $17 million, grossed $155 million at the box office, marking Candy's most successful movie since *Uncle Buck*.

However, in an October 6, 2023, interview, Malik Yoba, who co-starred with Candy in *Cool Runnings*, recalled a poignant conversation with the comedian. Candy confided that he had never taken a significant break in his career out of fear that Hollywood would forget about him. Yoba remembered:

He was 42 at that point and had never taken a vacation in his professional career. He said it was because he was afraid he'd never work again. That always stuck with me. At that time, he was probably the biggest he had ever been in his life, and I recall he had a trainer on set with him, and he was really struggling to lose weight. He was very insecure about his place in the Hollywood ecosystem. Most people would never imagine that would be the case for the great John Candy–but it was.

Director Jon Turteltaub echoed these sentiments, noting, "I know he had fears about his career and how he was perceived by people. His whole life, John hated not being liked. He was afraid of it on a personal and professional level. That eats away at a person."

Tragically, John Candy passed away on March 4, 1994, at the age of just 43, in Durango, Mexico, while filming *Wagons East*—a movie he was reportedly unhappy about doing. At the time of his death, Candy weighed approximately 330 pounds and smoked a pack of cigarettes a day. He had also endured long hours on set in very hot weather. In the docuseries *Autopsy: John Candy*, forensic pathologist Dr. Michael Hunter revealed that Candy was prone to binge eating in response to professional stress and setbacks.

Over the years, Hughes had mended fences with a few people he had distanced himself from, and Candy was likely to be on that list. However, Hughes never got the chance to reconcile with his old friend, and this loss weighed heavily on him.

In 1989, Hughes had purchased a farm in western Illinois near the Wisconsin border, which he named Redwing Farms. Although it was barren when he acquired it, he had big plans for the property someday. With Candy's death in 1994, that "someday" arrived sooner than expected. Hughes moved his family to a new home in Lake Forest, Illinois, and set up his company, Hughes Entertainment, in the New Trier West High School building, where he had filmed *Uncle Buck* and *Home Alone*. He spent much of his time on the farm, semi-retired from Hollywood.

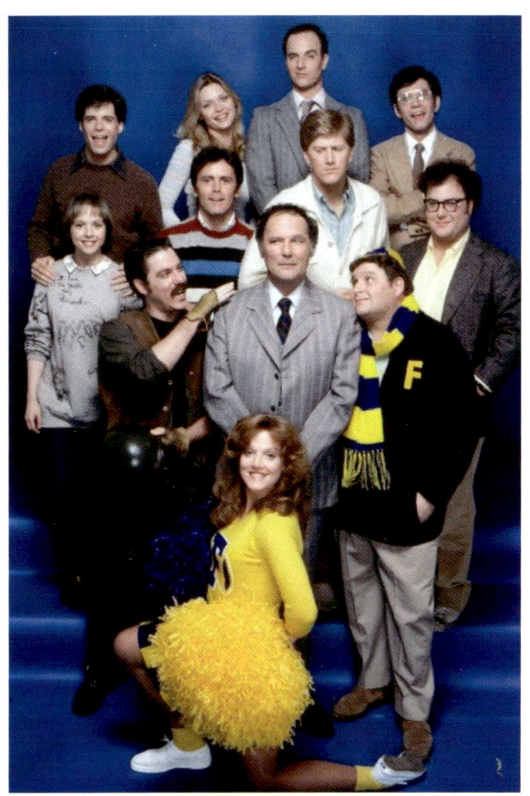

Michelle Pfeiffer in ABC's *Delta House*, 1979. (*ABC Network*)

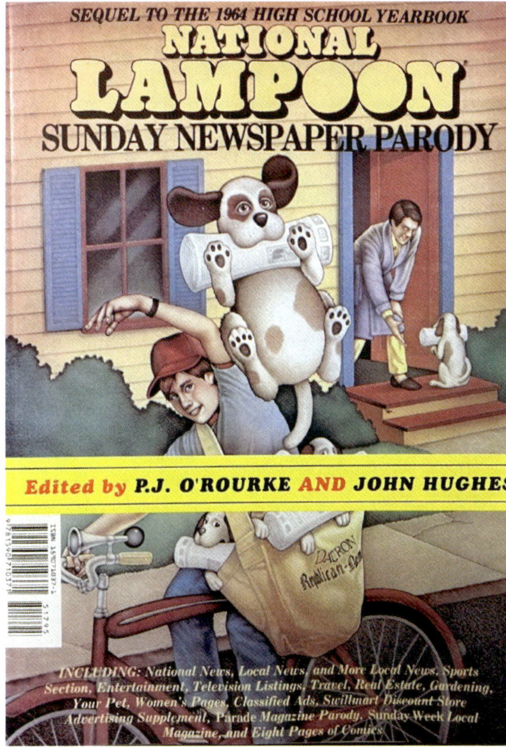

National Lampoon Sunday Newspaper Parody, 1978. (*National Lampoon*)

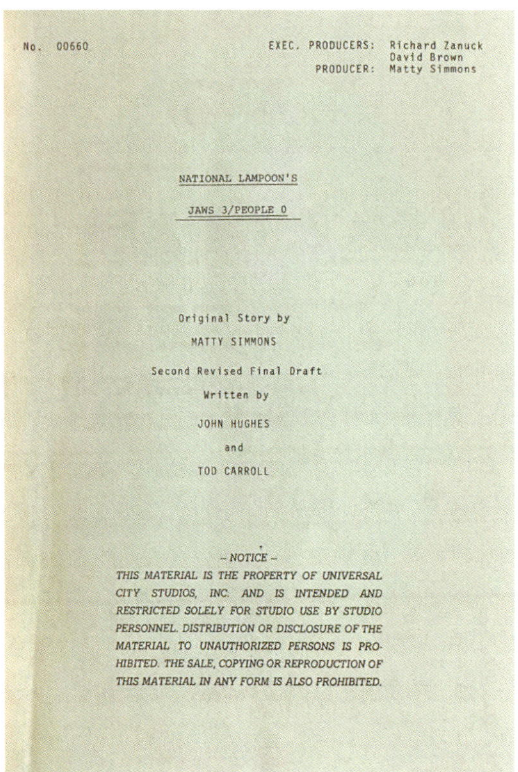

Jaws 3/People 0 first page "Written by," 1979. (*Universal Studios*)

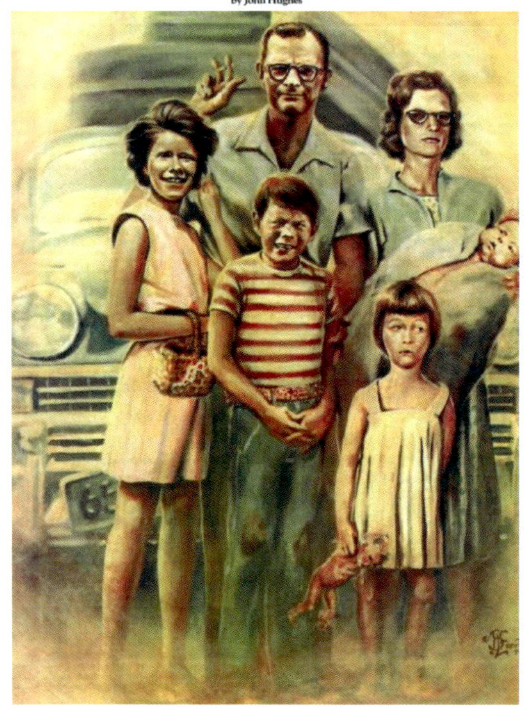

"Vacation '58," from *National Lampoon*, September 1979. (*National Lampoon*)

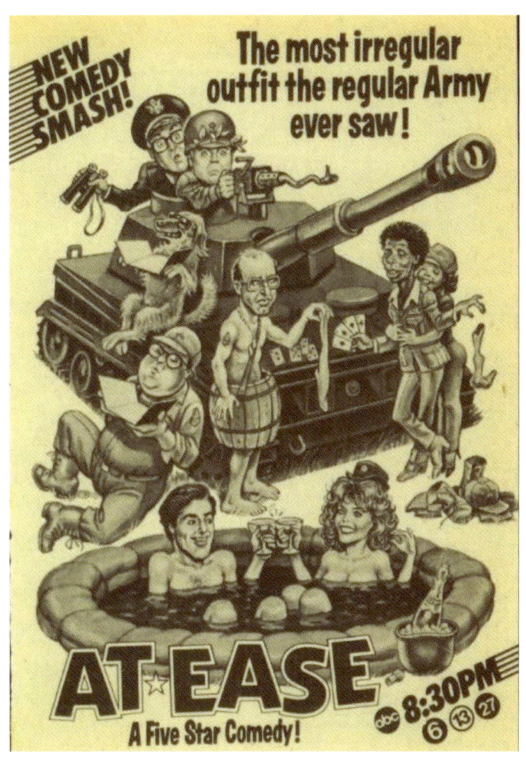

At Ease, TV Guide Promo, 1983. (*TV Guide*)

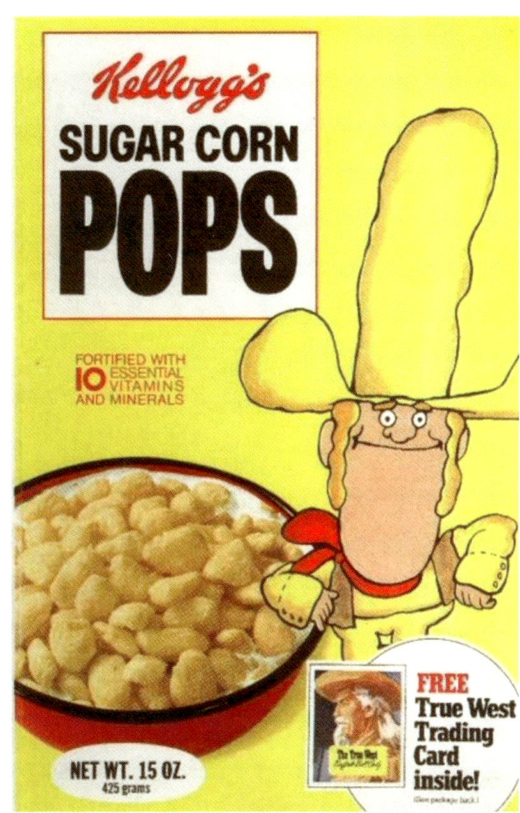

Big Yella, Sugar Corn Pops ad, 1979/80. (*Kellogg's*)

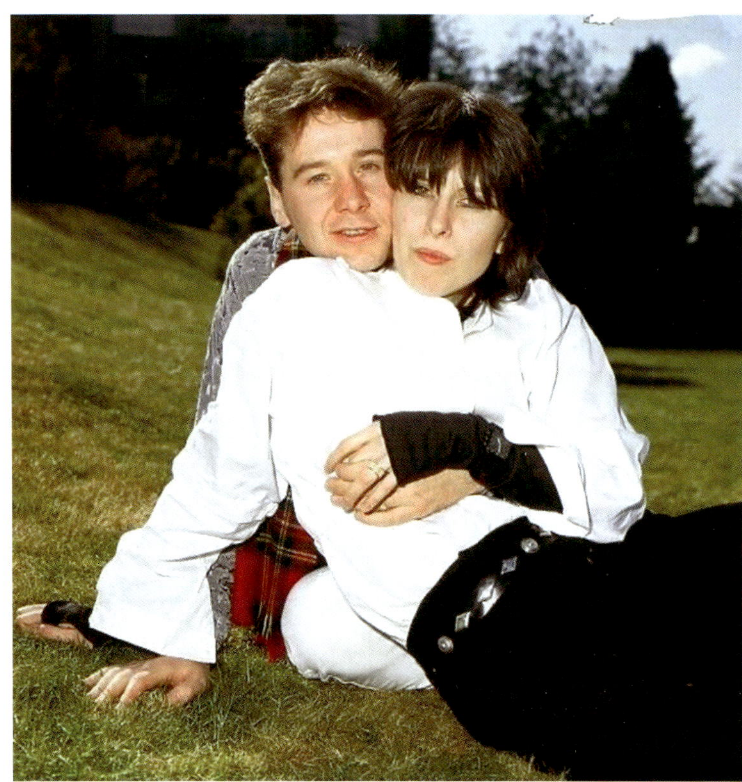

Jim Kerr
and Chrissie
Hynde,
July 1989.
(*Mirropix*)

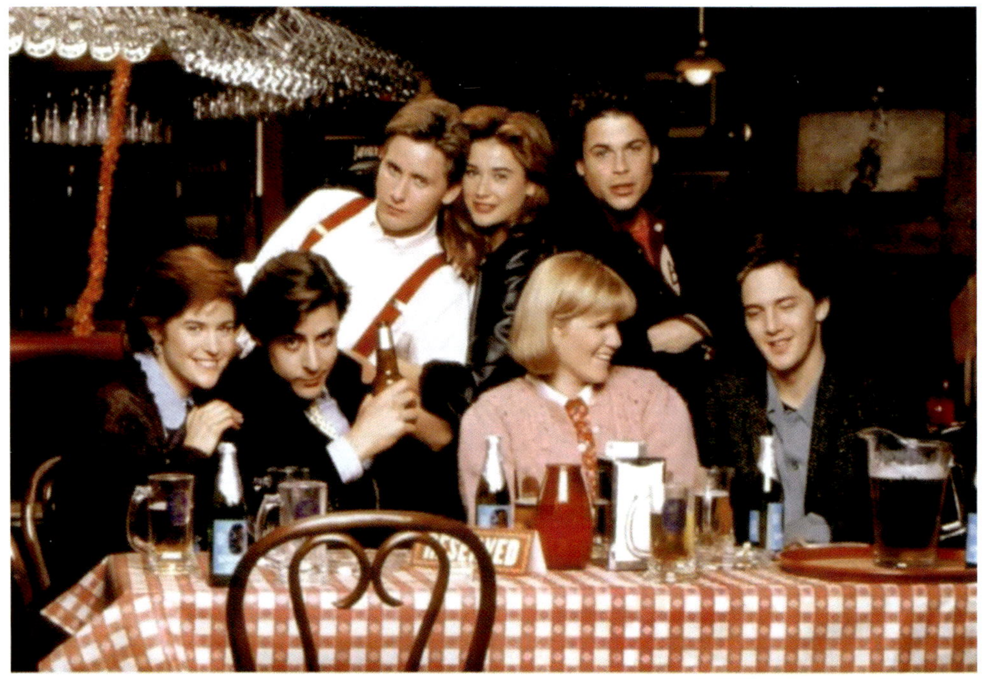

Ally Sheedy, Judd Nelson, Emilio Estevez, Demi Moore, Mare Winningham, Rob Lowe, and Andrew McCarthy, 1985. (*Columbia Pictures*)

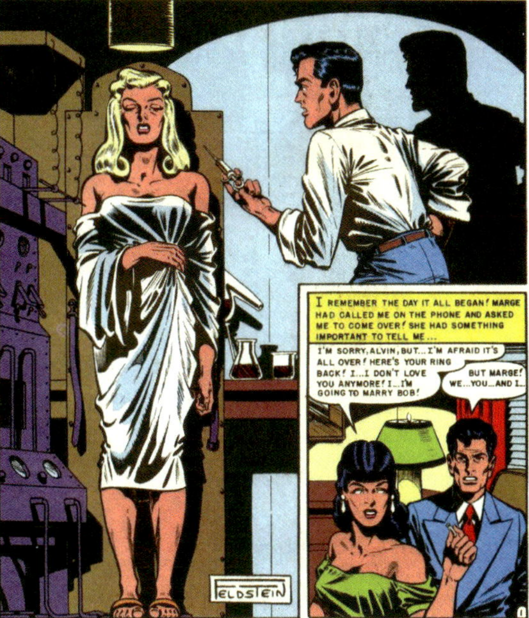

"Made of the Future" in *Weird Science* comics, January 1951. (*Al Felstein / EC Comics*)

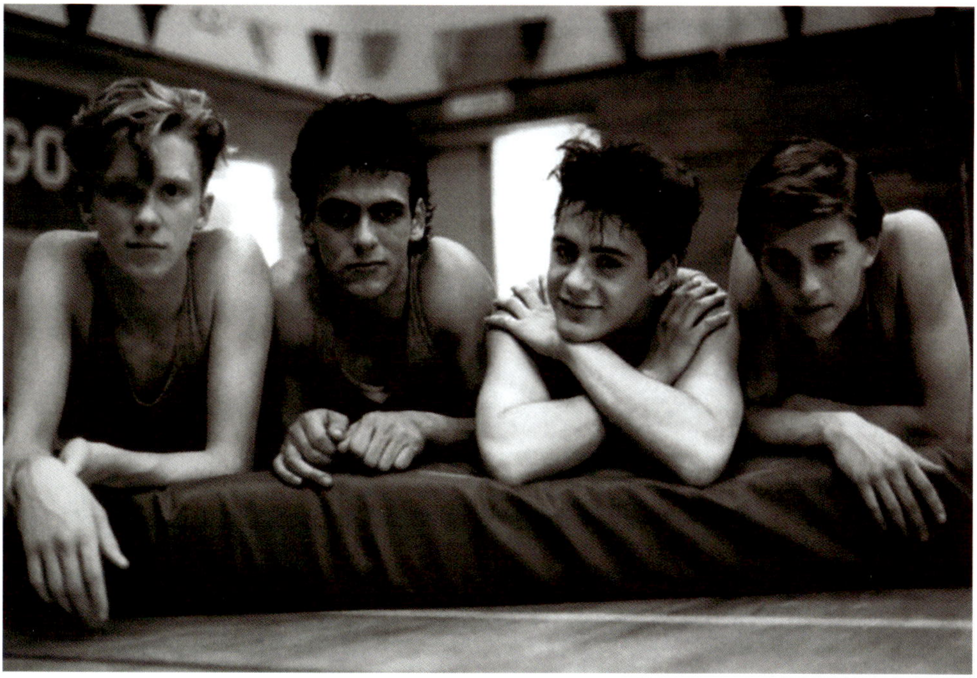

L-R: Anthony Michael Hall, Robert Rusler, Robert Downey Jr., and Ilan Mitchell-Smith, *Weird Science*, 1985. (*Hulton Archive*)

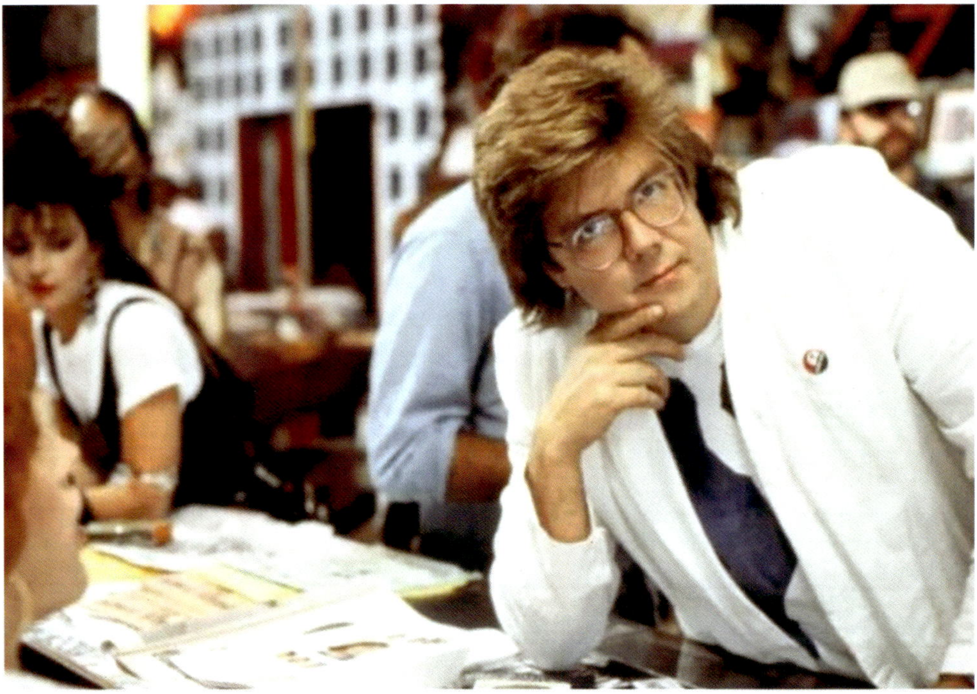

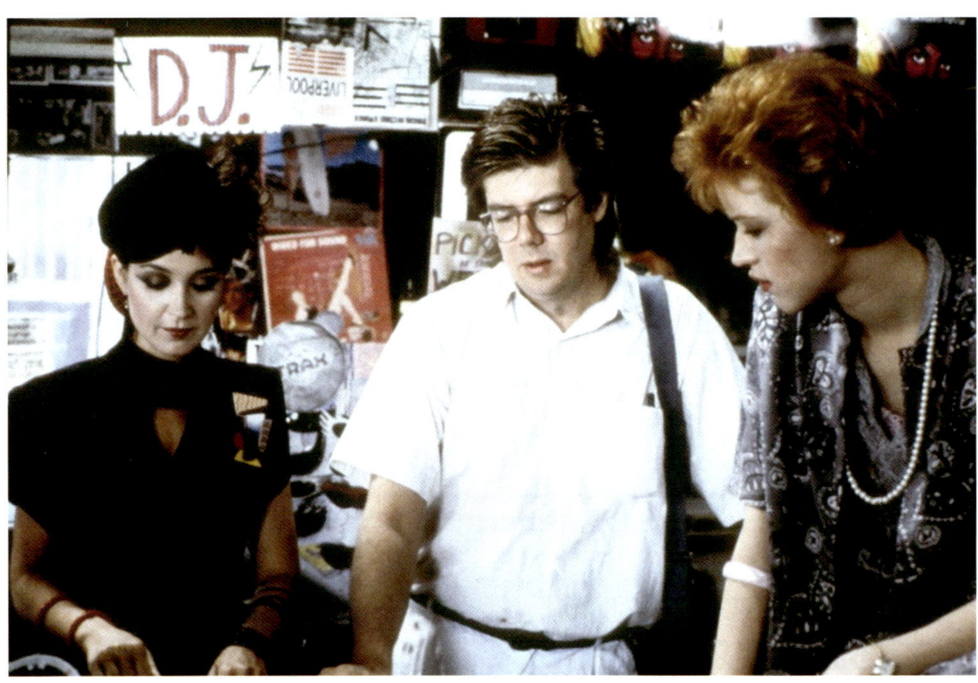

John Hughes, *Pretty in Pink*, 1986. (*Paramount Pictures*)

Annie Potts, John Hughes, and Molly Ringwald on the set of *Pretty in Pink*, 1986. (*Paramount Pictures*)

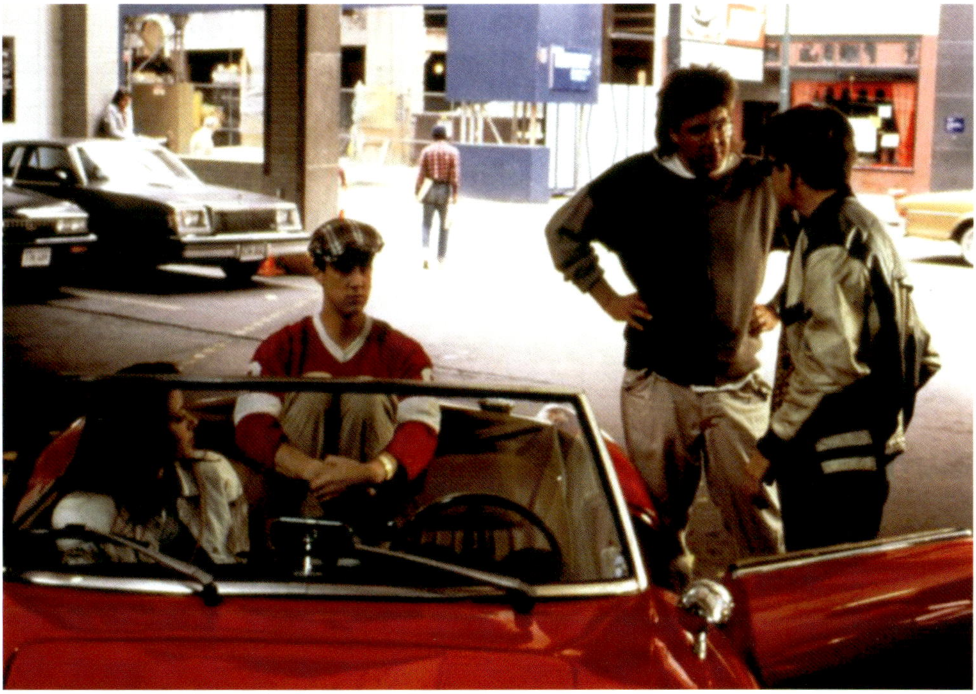

Mia Sara, Alan Ruck, John Hughes, and Matthew Broderick on the set of *Ferris Bueller's Day Off*, 1986. (*Paramount Pictures*)

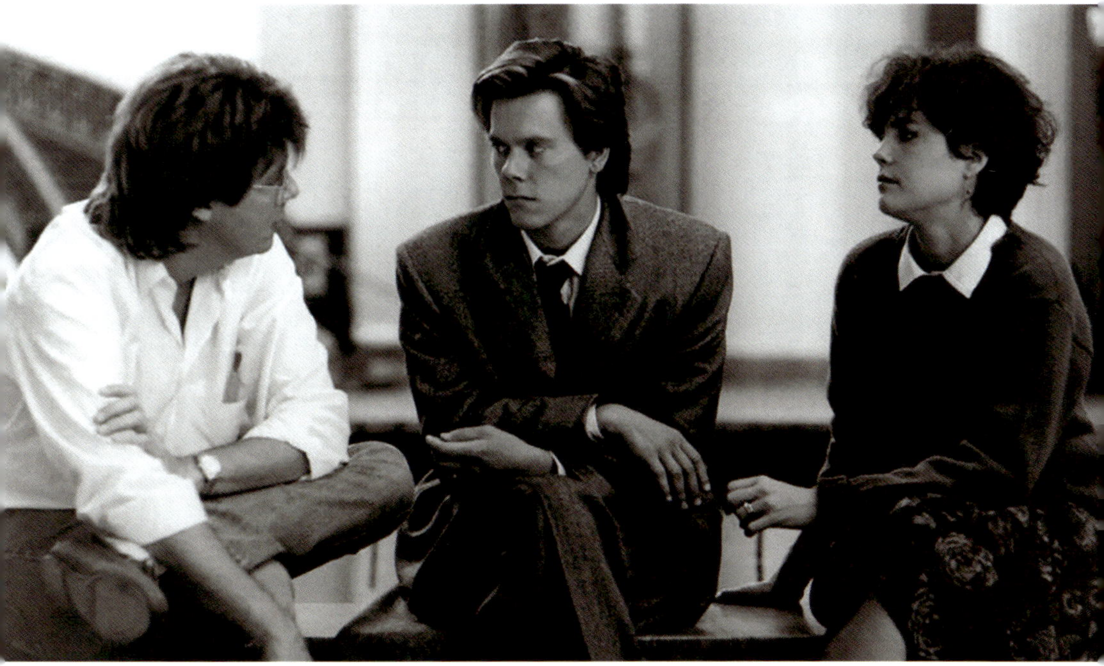

John Hughes, Kevin Bacon, and Elizabeth McGovern on the set of *She's Having a Baby*, 1988. (*Paramount Pictures*)

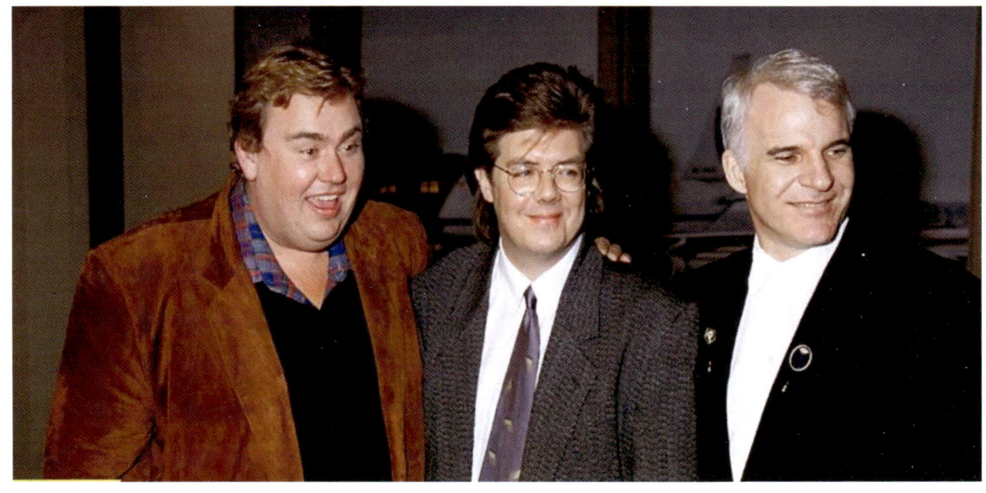

John Candy, John Hughes, and Steve Martin, 1988. (*Paramount Pictures*)

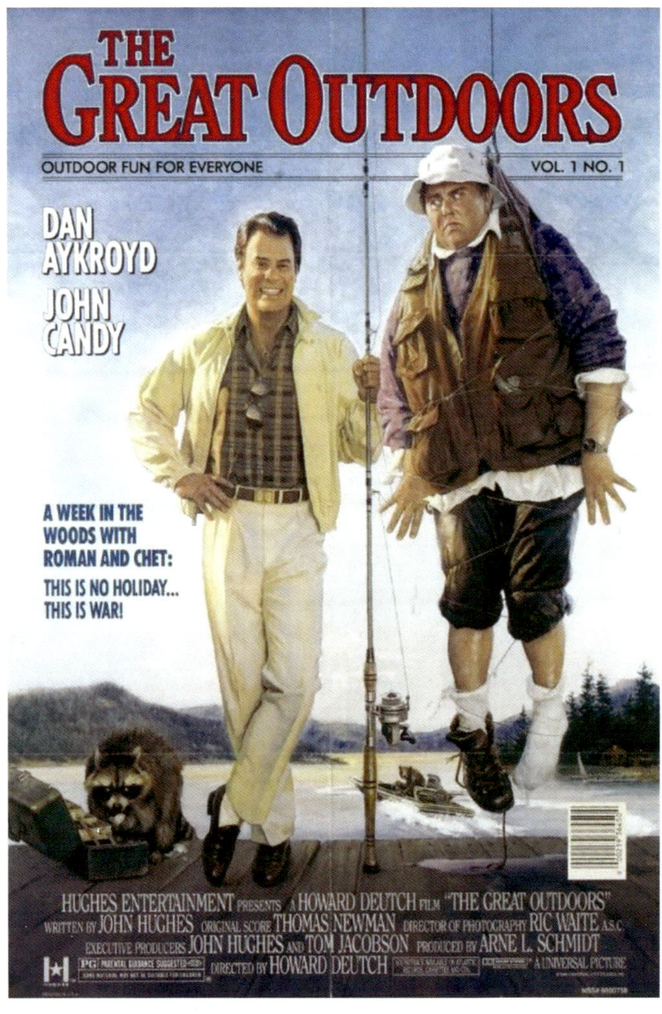

The Great Outdoors movie poster, 1988. (*Universal Pictures*)

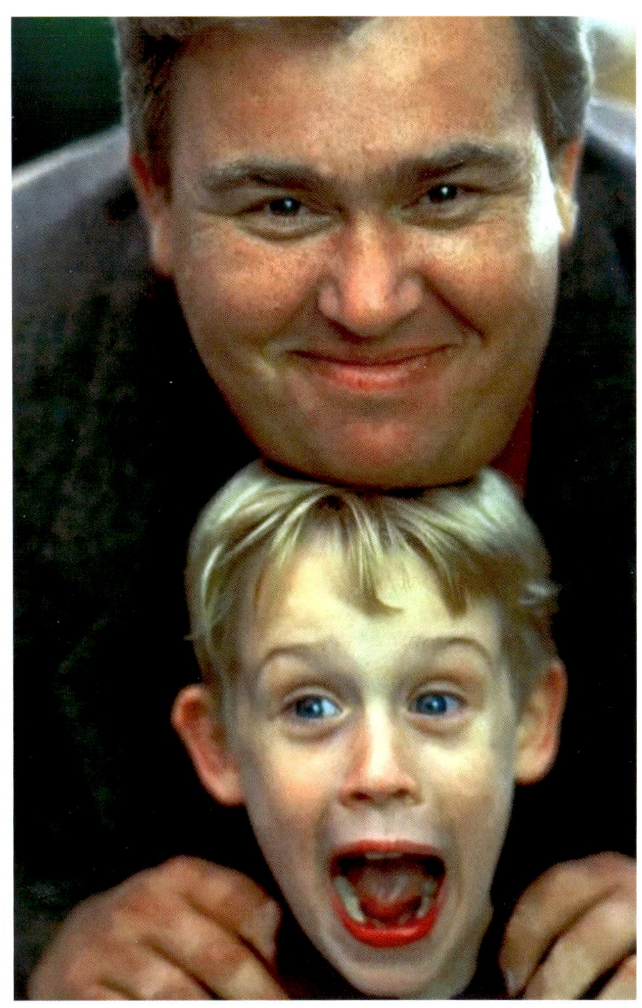

John Candy and
Macaulay Culkin on the
set of *Uncle Buck*, 1989.
(*Everett*)

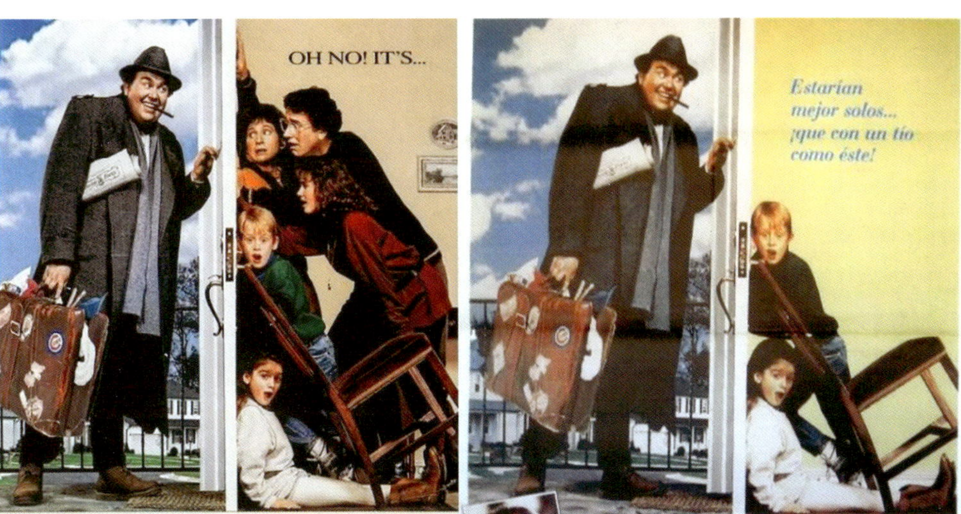

Uncle Buck movie poster and VHS poster, 1989. (*Universal Pictures*)

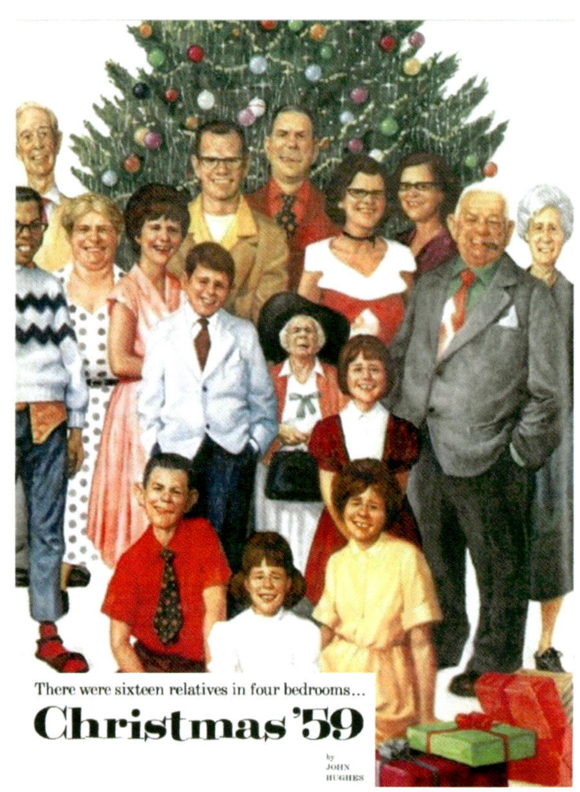

"Christmas '59," from *National Lampoon*, December 1980. (*National Lampoon, Inc.*)

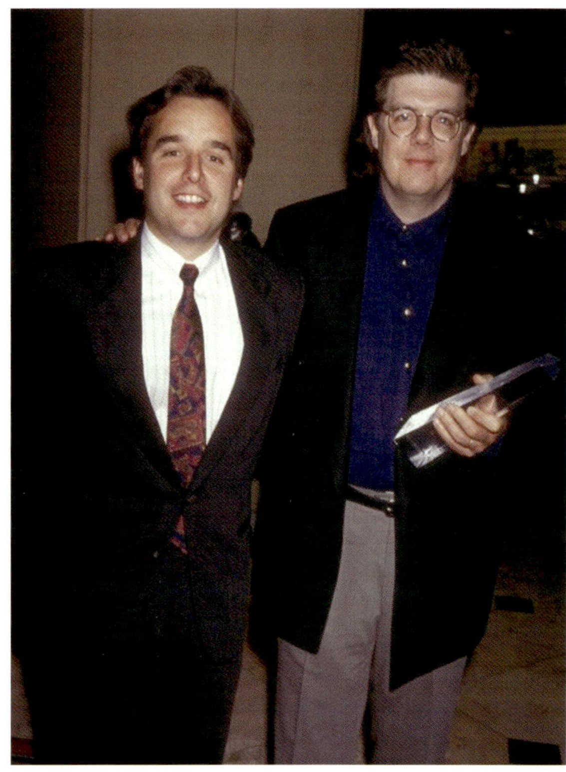

Chris Columbus and John Hughes attend ShoWest '91 Convention, 1991. (*Ron Galella Collection*)

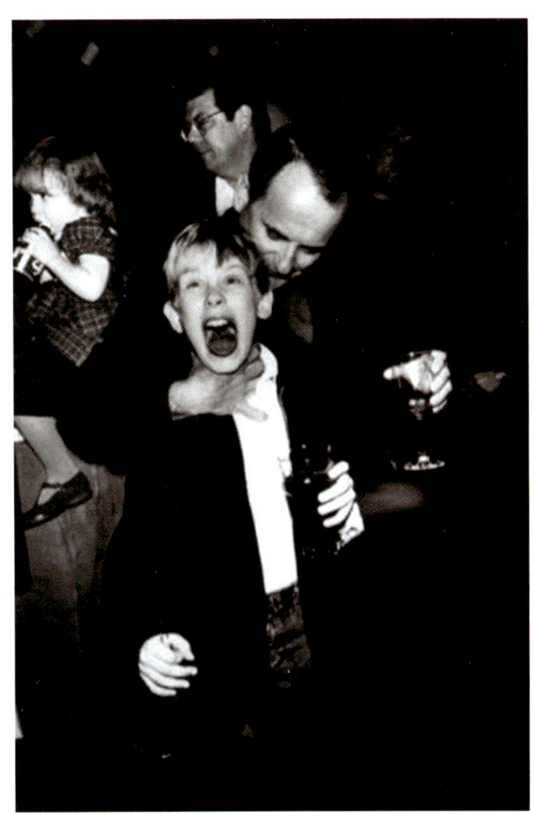

John Hughes, Macaulay Culkin, and Joe Pesci, *Home Alone* wrap party, 1990. (*Shotonwhat*)

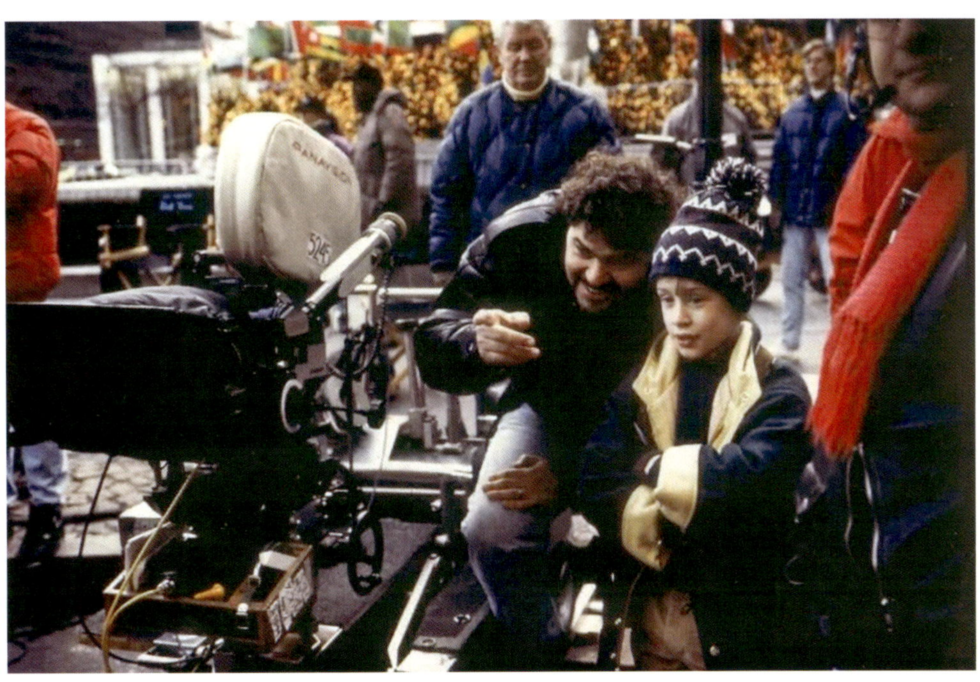

Cinematographer Julio Macat and Macaulay Culkin on the set of *Home Alone*, 1990. (*Macat*)

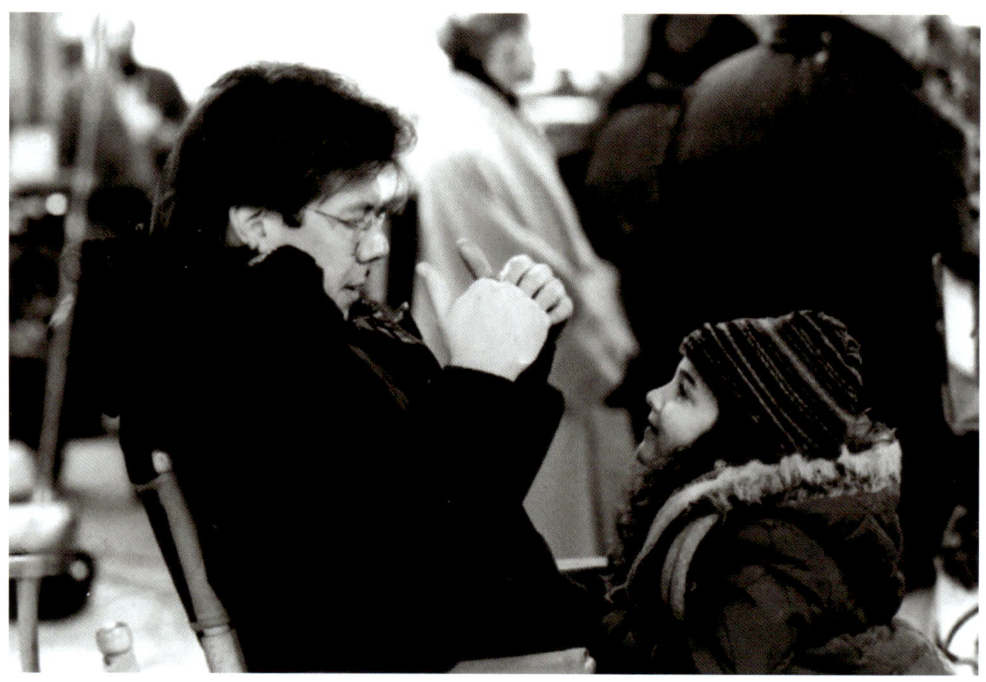

John Hughes and Alisan Porter on the set of *Curly Sue*, 1991. (*Colaimages*)

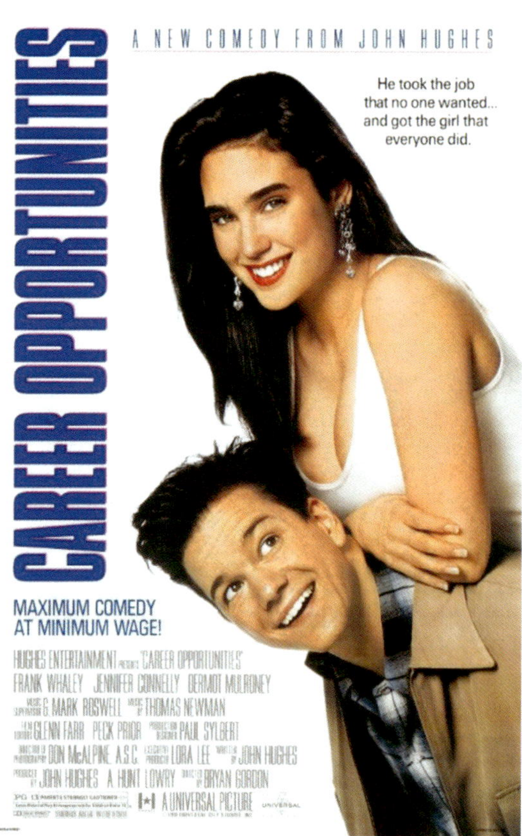

Frank Whaley and Jennifer Connelly, *Career Opportunities* poster, 1991. (*Universal*)

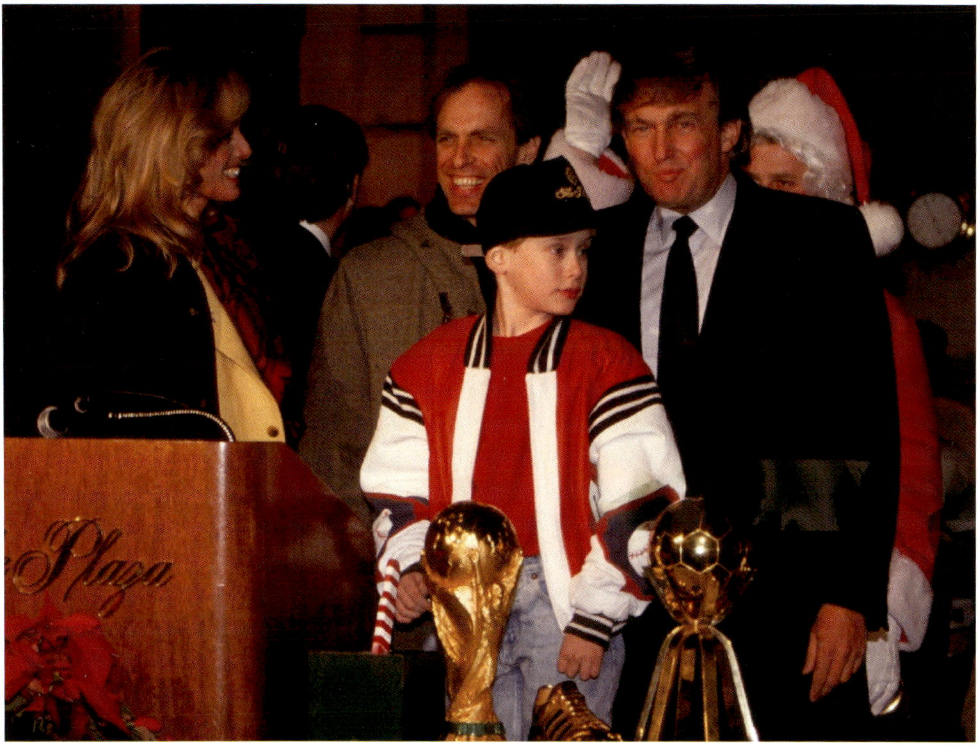

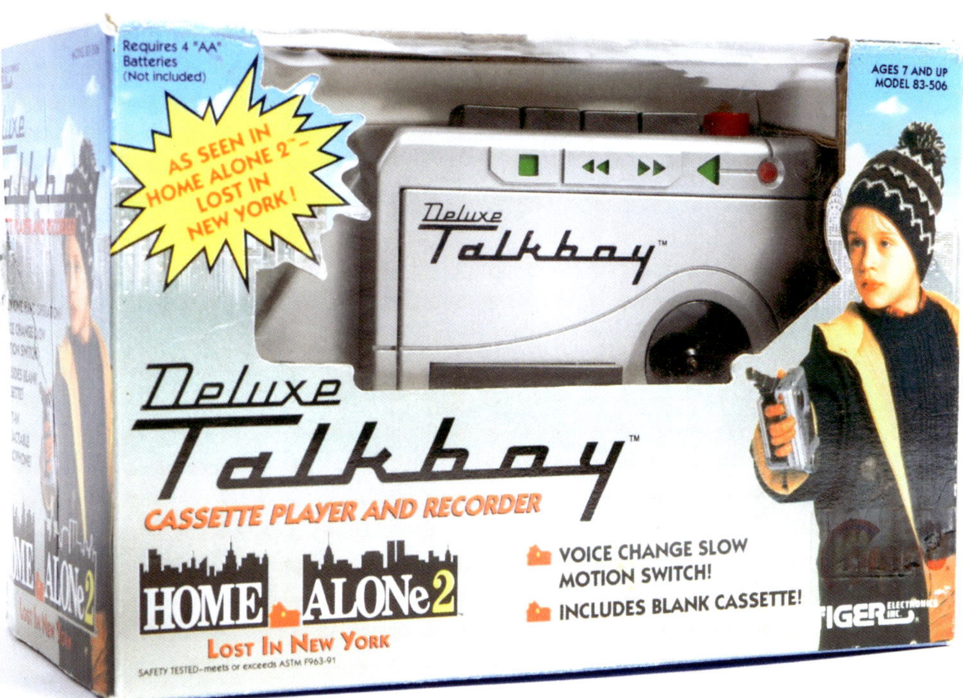

Macaulay Culkin and Donald Trump, *Home Alone 2*, 1992. (*20th Century Fox*)

Talkboy from *Home Alone 2*. (*Tiger Toys*)

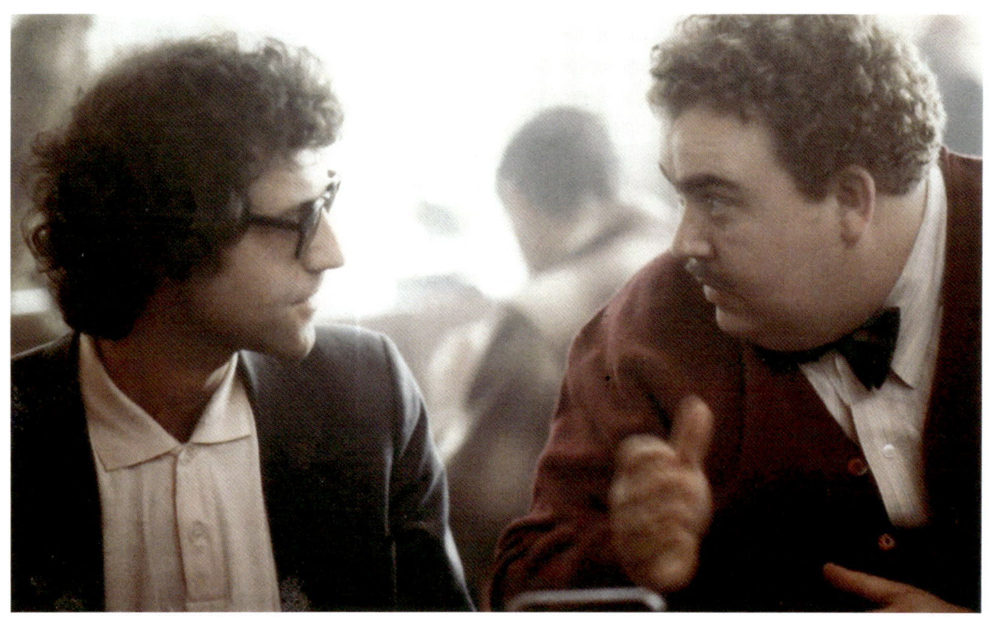

Tarquin Gotch and John Candy on the set of *Planes, Trains and Automobiles*, 1988. (*Demon Music Group*)

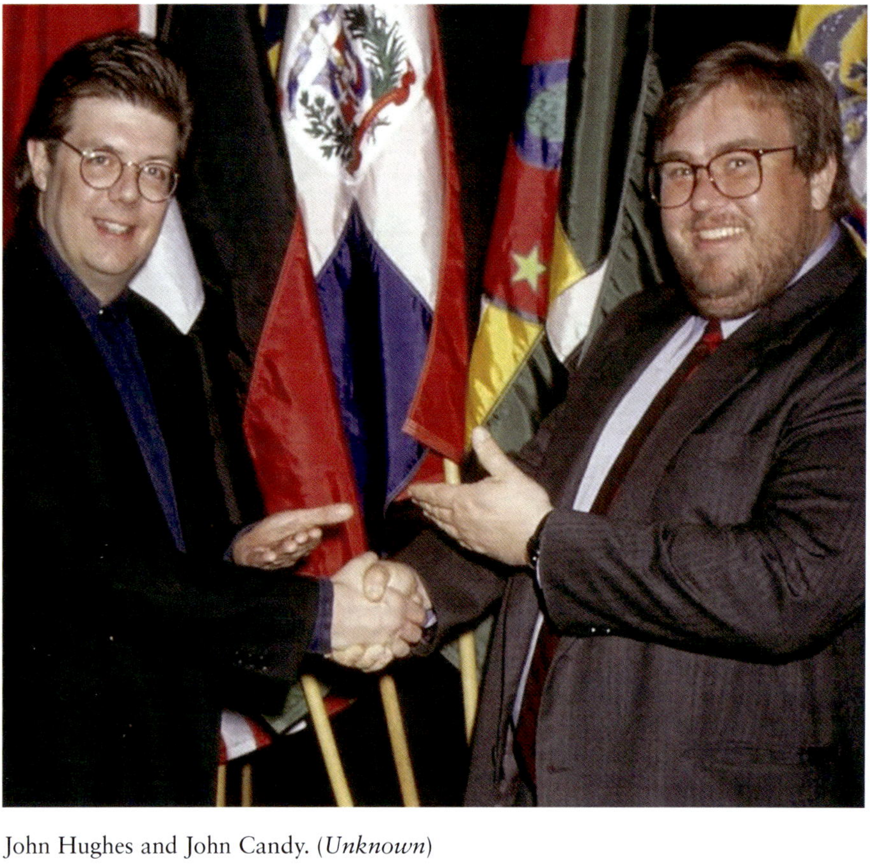

John Hughes and John Candy. (*Unknown*)

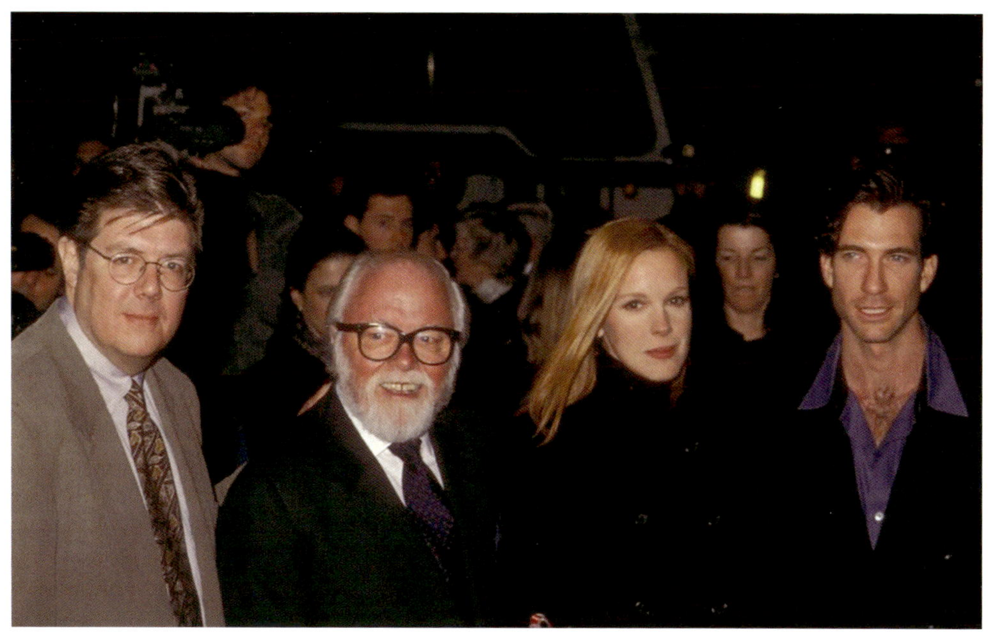

John Hughes, Richard Attenborough, Elizabeth Perkins, and Dylan McDermott, opening of *Miracle on 34th Street*, 1994. (*20th Century Fox*)

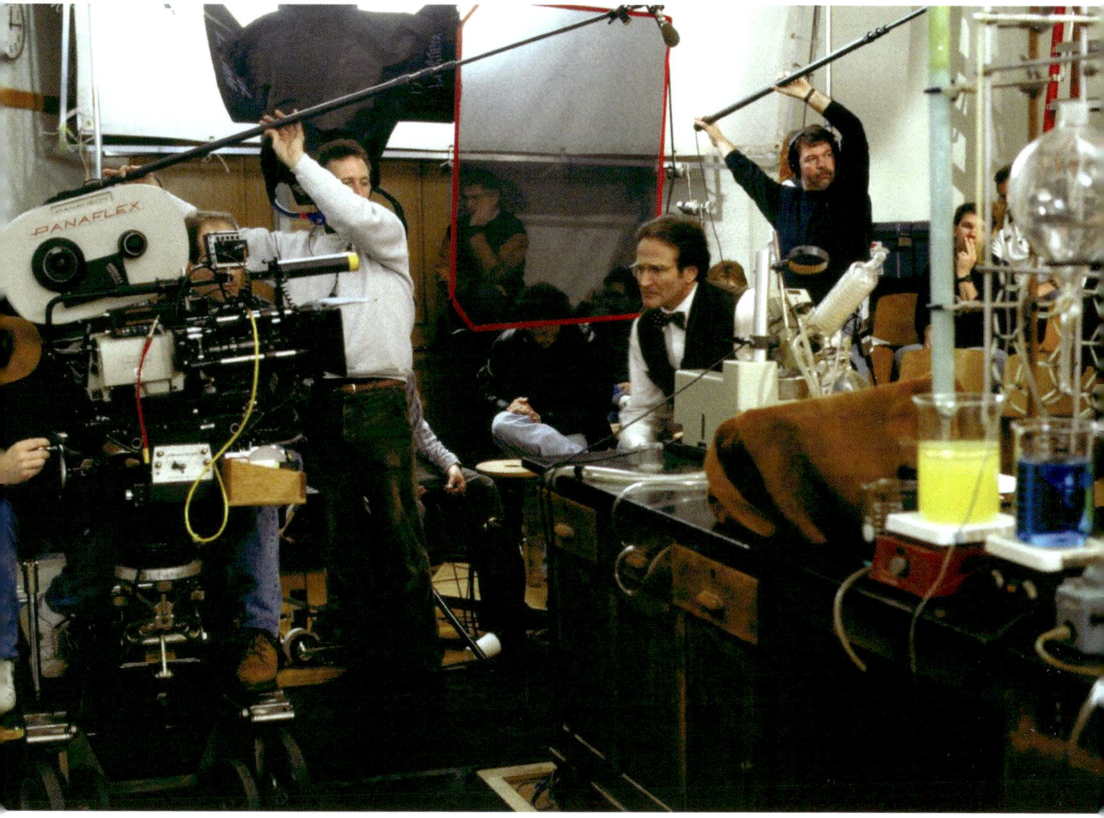

Director Les Mayfield and Robin Williams shooting *Flubber*, 1997. (*Walt Disney Pictures*)

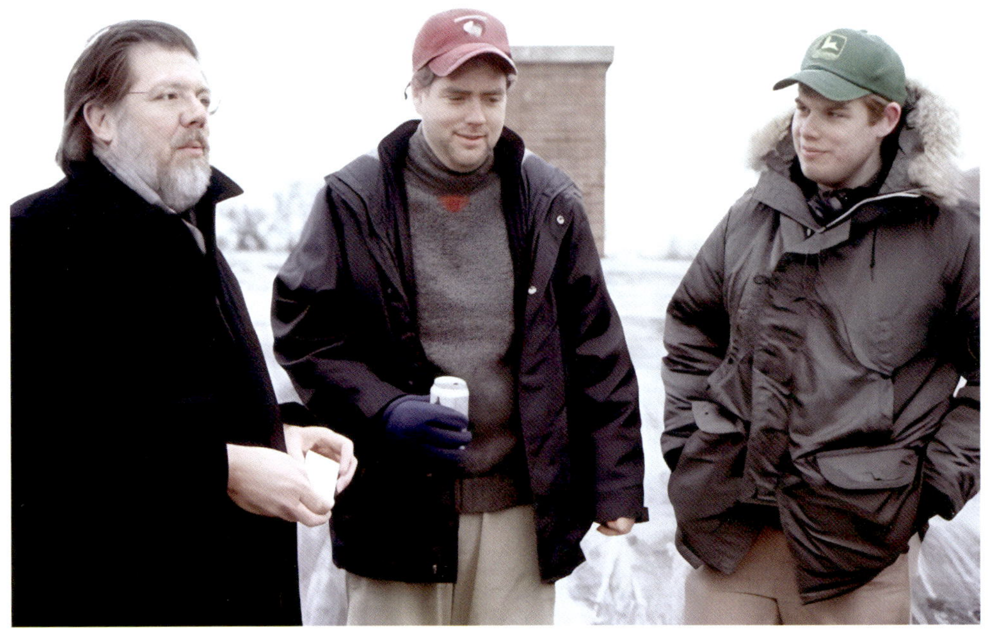

John Hughes, Kyle Cooper, and Hughes's son James Hughes on the set of *New Port South*, 2001. (*Touchstone Pictures*)

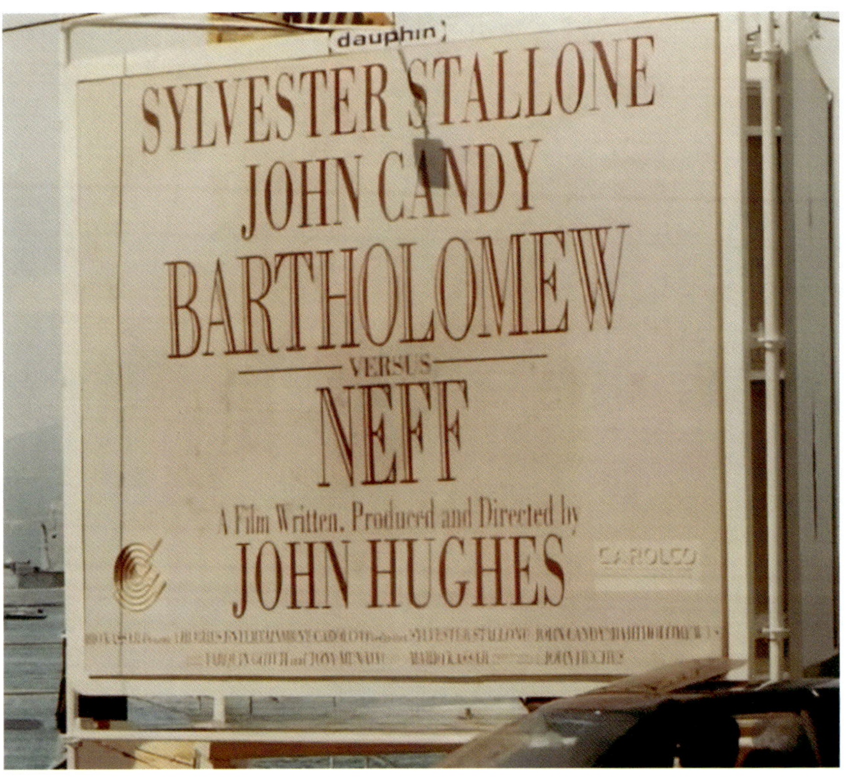

Bartholomew vs. Neff billboard, 1990. (*Carolco Pictures*)

Whether he withdrew to avoid a fate similar to Candy's—given his own workaholic tendencies and smoking habit—or because he harbored some guilt over his friend's death, Hughes's retreat marked the end of an era in both his career and his life.

After returning to Chicago, John Hughes developed a close friendship with actor Vince Vaughn. The two would often engage in long, late-night conversations. Vaughn recalls Hughes confiding that he left Hollywood because he was deeply concerned about the impact it was having on his sons. He feared that the industry's influence would cause them to lose sight of what truly mattered and distort their understanding of happiness. Vaughn also shared a poignant story Hughes told him—one of the key reasons he decided to walk away from it all was his belief that Hollywood had "killed" his friend John Candy by relentlessly overworking him.

Although Hughes had lost interest in directing films, he couldn't stop his relentless writing. He continued to produce and oversee films, but these projects were no longer fueled by passion; he was simply going through the motions.

23

Miracle on 34th Street

Hughes had already started to lose trust in Hollywood and was contemplating stepping back after the lukewarm reception of *Curly Sue*. The situation worsened with the disappointing outcome of *Baby's Day Out*, but John Candy's death was the final straw. Hughes began retreating from the industry, shifting from creating original characters and plotlines to rewriting old movie scripts. Though he continued producing films, his heart was no longer in it.

With a standing commitment to 20th Century Fox and a proven track record with Christmas-themed films, the studio approached Hughes about rewriting and remaking the 1947 classic, *Miracle on 34th Street*. Hughes agreed, and the project quickly moved forward, with Les Mayfield hired as the director in November 1993. Hughes had initially wanted Mayfield to direct *Baby's Day Out*, but due to Mayfield's prior commitment to a Disney project, Hughes gave him another opportunity with *Miracle on 34th Street*.

Hughes envisioned the remake as both an homage to the 1947 original and a fresh take on the story. As a lover of classic films, Hughes described himself as the "guardian of this classic American story" in a November 6, 1994, interview. He mentioned that while he had made changes, they were subtle enough that audiences wouldn't notice.

For the film's cinematography, Hughes brought in Julio Macat, who had worked with him since *Home Alone*. Hughes wanted the film to have the ability to be viewed in color or black and white, achieving a visual continuity with the original. Macat delivered on this vision, ensuring the lighting could seamlessly transition between the two formats.

Principal photography on *Miracle on 34th Street* began on April 7, 1994, and concluded on June 29, 1994. Mara Wilson, fresh off her success in *Mrs. Doubtfire*, was cast as Susan Walker. She came recommended by Chris Columbus, who had worked with her on *Mrs. Doubtfire*. Although Wilson and her mother liked Hughes, they grew concerned during production as it became evident that Hughes was less than involved, likely still grieving Candy's death.

In April 1994, the *Los Angeles Times* reported that Macy's had refused to allow the use of their name in the remake. A Macy's spokesperson stated, "We feel the original stands on its own and could not be improved upon." As a result, the production had to recreate their own version of the Macy's Thanksgiving Day Parade, naming the store in the film "Cole's" instead.

Miracle on 34th Street premiered on November 15, 1994, at Radio City Music Hall and was released nationwide three days later. It opened in eighth place for the weekend box office and was the third most successful of the new releases, including the first *Star Trek: The Next Generation* film. Ultimately, the film grossed only $17 million, less than its original budget, and finished eighty-second for the year. However, VHS sales during the following holiday season helped boost its earnings to around $47 million.

Critics were quick to compare the remake to the original, noting the absence of Macy's and how it impacted the film's authenticity. Hughes admitted in interviews that he was initially disappointed by Macy's refusal, particularly when forced to recreate the parade in Manhattan's Upper West Side. However, he later acknowledged in a November 18, 1994, *New York Times* interview that it was a blessing in disguise, allowing him to create a family-oriented store that evoked the charm of the original.

24

101 Dalmatians and *Flubber*

In 1992, Joe Roth, the executive who championed John Hughes' vision with *Home Alone*, left 20th Century Fox to establish an independent production company at Walt Disney Studios.

By 1993, Jeffrey Katzenberg was the powerhouse at Disney, credited with revitalizing their motion-picture division through adult-oriented comedies at Touchstone Pictures and launching successful TV shows like *The Golden Girls* and *Home Improvement*. He also played a key role in reviving Disney's animation department with modern classics like *The Little Mermaid* and *Beauty and the Beast*.

Despite his successes, Katzenberg's increasingly difficult demeanor made him unpopular with several Disney executives, including Roy E. Disney, nephew of Walt Disney, and CEO Michael Eisner. In October 1993, Katzenberg expected to be promoted to president of the company, but Eisner, who was close to then president Frank Wells, promised Katzenberg the position only if Wells were no longer with Disney. Tragically, six months later, Wells died in a helicopter crash, yet Katzenberg's anticipated promotion never materialized. Frustrated, Katzenberg left Disney and, in October 1994, teamed up with Steven Spielberg and David Geffen to form DreamWorks. Following Katzenberg's departure, Eisner appointed Joe Roth as chief of The Walt Disney Studios. One of Roth's first moves was to strike a deal with John Hughes.

Despite leaving Paramount after *She's Having a Baby*, Hughes maintained a friendly relationship with producer Ricardo Mestres. Mestres was later appointed president of Hollywood Pictures, a Disney label. After a string of box office failures, Mestres resigned in 1994 but was retained by Disney under a long-term production deal.

In 1995, Hughes began winding down his Hughes Entertainment banner and, on February 19, 1995, announced a partnership with Ricardo Mestres to form a new company under the Disney umbrella called Great Oaks Entertainment. The name was inspired by the saying, "Great oaks from small acorns grow." The new company planned to produce films and television shows, publish works, and explore interactive projects. Hughes would remain based in Chicago, Mestres in L.A., and Bill Ryan, who had worked with Hughes since *Dennis the Menace*, would be based in London.

In 1993, Hughes traveled to London to scout British comedy talent for future projects. He met with Rowan Atkinson, Hugh Laurie, and Harry Enfield, seeking to learn from them, as he mentioned in a rare interview later that year. Hughes and Mestres also announced a thirteen-episode commitment for an untitled sitcom with NBC, but the project never came to fruition.

At that time, Hughes had six films lined up with Disney and four more at 20th Century Fox. Mestres had two projects in development at New Line, giving their new venture, Great Oaks Entertainment, a robust start with twelve projects across three studios. These included potential sequels to *Dennis the Menace* and *Vacation* at Warner Brothers.

The first film Hughes and Mestres chose to produce through Disney was a live-action remake of the classic 1961 Disney animated film, *101 Dalmatians*. Following the success of Disney's live-action *Jungle Book*, the studio was eager to mine its animated library for more live-action adaptations. Hughes completed the 128-page script in just one month, and Joe Roth described it as having the same spirit as *Home Alone*.

In a 1996 interview promoting the film, Hughes explained, "It wasn't so much the story; it was simply the notion of doing a Disney film." With Hughes's track record and his new partnership with Disney, the budget was set at an impressive $67 million.

Despite Hughes's hesitation about taking on such a monumental project during a period when he was feeling increasingly disillusioned with Hollywood, he approached the film with one key principle: it had to be a Disney movie, not a John Hughes movie. In a December 1, 1996 interview with *SFGate* magazine, Hughes shared his mindset: "I approached it as if Walt Disney himself had come up to me in 1959 or '60, and he gave me this book and said, 'Look, we know you can't draw, so what would you do to make a live-action movie out of it?'"

Before writing the screenplay, Hughes read the original book by Dodie Smith and repeatedly watched the 1961 animated film. He decided that this time, the animals would not speak, even though Jim Henson's Creature Shop, which had successfully created talking animals for *Babe* in 1995, could have done the same for *101 Dalmatians*. Hughes believed that more realism in a fantasy setting would make the story more relatable for the audience. Adapting a classic animated film into live-action proved to be a more complex task than remaking *Miracle on 34th Street*.

Hughes particularly enjoyed writing the character of Cruella de Vil. Used to creating bumbling villains, he relished the chance to craft a backstory for a genuinely evil character, something the animated version had never explored. After seeing Glenn Close perform on Broadway in *Sunset Boulevard*, Hughes believed she was perfect for the role of Cruella.

In a 1996 press kit, Hughes mentioned that, while he couldn't stop writing and would likely direct again someday, he felt a director with experience in large-scale productions was needed for this project. He chose Stephen Herek, a Disney studio director in the 1990s, known for films like *Bill and Ted's Excellent Adventure*, *The Mighty Ducks*, and *The Three Musketeers*.

With Great Oaks Entertainment now operating in London, the decision was made to film *101 Dalmatians* there. Principal photography began on October 22, 1995, and wrapped on January 21, 1996. The film had three premieres: in New York on November 18, 1996, in Hollywood on November 24, 1996, and at Royal Albert Hall in London on December 4, 1996. It opened nationwide in the U.S. on the Wednesday before Thanksgiving, November 27, 1996.

Grossing $46 million in its first weekend, *101 Dalmatians* dominated the box office and broke the Thanksgiving weekend record. It even surpassed the new *Star Trek* movie. The film ended the year in eighth place, earning $121 million domestically and $320 million overall after its VHS release in April 1997.

Critics like Roger Ebert, Owen Gleiberman, and Kenneth Turan noted the film's distinctively Hughesian style, particularly the bumbling villains reminiscent of Harry and Marv from *Home Alone*. Janet Maslin offered a glowing review.

Despite recent misfires like *Baby's Day Out* and *Miracle on 34th Street*, *101 Dalmatians* marked a triumphant return for Hughes. Not only did the film succeed at the box office, but Hughes also made more money than ever before by securing a share of the merchandising profits. Joe Roth remarked that *101 Dalmatians* was the first test of whether Disney could promote a live-action film as effectively as its animated classics—and it was a resounding success.

While preparing *101 Dalmatians*, Hughes and Disney also decided to remake another 1961 Disney film, this time the live-action classic *The Absent-Minded Professor*. Unlike *Miracle on 34th Street*, which was a cherished holiday film, remaking *The Absent-Minded Professor* seemed like a more practical idea. The original starred Fred MacMurray and was shot in black and white. While the special effects were cutting-edge for their time, thirty years later Industrial Light & Magic was available to significantly enhance them.

When Joe Roth joined Disney in 1992, he had a mandate to produce at least twenty-five films over five years. By the time Hughes came on board with Great Oaks, Roth had only produced seven, so remaking older films was a viable strategy. Roth approached Hughes about writing and producing a remake of *The Absent-Minded Professor*, and Hughes agreed, reimagining the film as *Flubber*.

Hughes wrote the script with Robin Williams in mind for the lead role. However, Williams had vowed never to work with Disney again after a dispute over the use of his voice in merchandise for the smash Disney hit *Aladdin*. Williams had even agreed to take a lower salary to prevent his voice work as the Genie from being used commercially, but Disney breached that agreement.

The feud became public when Williams criticized Disney on the *Today* show in 1993 while promoting Chris Columbus' *Mrs. Doubtfire*. Williams refused to work with Disney again until they issued an apology. While Disney's then president Jeffrey Katzenberg never apologized, his successor, Joe Roth, did, and Williams accepted. Williams not only reprised his role as the Genie in the third *Aladdin* film (after being recast in the second) but also accepted the role in *Flubber* that Hughes had written for him. Les Mayfield, who had directed *Miracle on 34th Street*, returned to direct *Flubber*.

Filming for *Flubber* began on October 8, 1996, in San Francisco, just a month before Hughes and Disney would find out how *101 Dalmatians* performed at the box office, and continued until February 4, 1997.

For the third time in three years, a Hughes remake was set to open on Thanksgiving weekend. *Flubber* debuted at number one at the box office, grossing $26 million in its opening weekend and outpacing *Alien: Resurrection* by $10 million.

Flubber ended up as the fifteenth highest-grossing film of 1997, in a year dominated by the release of *Titanic*. It grossed over \$177 million worldwide. As the *Los Angeles Times* noted on November 29, 1997, "There's no question that *Flubber* is a big movie. How big? Even if Disney's fondest wishes come true, this holiday weekend has nothing on last year's, when *101 Dalmatians* became the highest-grossing Thanksgiving opener ever."

Once again, Hughes found himself chasing the success of his past efforts.

Critics were harsh on *Flubber*, with many questioning Hughes' continued reliance on the *Home Alone* formula of slapstick humor involving bumbling villains. The Washington Post remarked in their November 28, 1997, review, "It was fresh when Joe Pesci and Daniel Stern were doing it seven years ago; it looks like overkill now."

Janet Maslin of *The New York Times* echoed this sentiment in her November 26, 1997, review, writing, "Thanks to John Hughes's head-bashing approach to children's comedy, *Flubber* is now more akin to a dangerous weapon."

Even though his films continued to perform well financially, the negative reviews began to take a toll on Hughes. Despite the success of both *101 Dalmatians* and *Flubber*, Hughes retreated further from Hollywood, spending more time at home in Chicago and on his farm.

While Disney went on to produce a sequel, *102 Dalmatians*, in 2000, Hughes had no involvement. A sequel to *Flubber* was never made, despite the original *The Absent-Minded Professor* spawning Disney's first-ever sequel, *Son of Flubber*, in 1963.

25

Home Alone 3

After *Miracle on 34th Street*, and having established Great Oaks Company with Disney, Hughes still had an obligation to deliver another film to Fox. While working on *101 Dalmatians* and *Flubber*, Hughes also began drafting a new installment of the *Home Alone* franchise. Originally, the plan was to film a third *Home Alone* immediately after the second, around 1993, with Macaulay Culkin reprising his role as a teenage Kevin.

At that time, Culkin was 13 and one of the biggest stars in the world. However, he had already committed to four films and was feeling burned out. By 1996, when Hughes and his team decided to move forward with another *Home Alone* film, Culkin had retired from acting.

Hughes had considered sequels for *The Breakfast Club*, *Ferris Bueller's Day Off*, *Vacation*, and even *Dennis the Menace*. He enjoyed exploring how his characters evolved over time. But *Home Alone 3* would prove to be a challenge. With Culkin out of the picture, Hughes initially planned to focus on the burglars, with Joe Pesci and Daniel Stern reprising their roles as Harry and Marv. He also considered centering the story on Kieran Culkin, Macaulay's real-life brother, who played Fuller, Kevin's cousin, in the previous films. The idea was that Fuller would be left home alone by his parents, Uncle Frank and his wife. However, Pesci, Stern, and even Kieran Culkin declined to participate.

Hughes initially asked Chris Columbus to return as director, but Columbus, not feeling comfortable working with an entirely new cast, suggested that the role should go to someone making their directorial debut, just as he had with the first *Home Alone*. This was a polite way of saying that after the box office success of *Mrs. Doubtfire*, he was ready to move on from the *Home Alone* franchise. However, Hughes took Columbus's advice and hired Raja Gosnell, the editor of the first two *Home Alone* films, to make his directorial debut with *Home Alone 3*.

Had Hughes not been obligated to fulfill his contract with Fox, he might have scrapped the film altogether. However, he wasn't ready to let go of the characters he had created and even considered spinning off Joe Pesci's character, Harry, into a standalone film. Unfortunately, Pesci was too busy with other projects, including *8 Heads in a Duffel Bag*, *Gone Fishin'*, and *Lethal Weapon 4*.

Hughes was so enthusiastic about his original characters that he even contemplated a spin-off for Daniel Stern's character, Marv, as well. Some believe this idea eventually evolved into the 1995 film *Bushwhacked*, another 20th Century Fox production, where Stern's character, posing as a scout leader to escape a false murder charge, endured physical comedy reminiscent of his role as Marv. However, Hughes had no involvement in that film.

There was also some consideration of turning *Home Alone 3* into a television pilot instead of a theatrical release, but Fox ultimately decided to proceed with it as a major motion picture.

With the original cast unwilling to return, Hughes wrote an entirely new screenplay featuring a different set of characters. *Home Alone 3* introduced a new family, the Pruitts, and was still set in Chicago, but unlike the previous films, the third installment was not set during Christmas, even though it was marketed as a holiday film.

The film featured Haviland Morris as the mother, who, interestingly enough, had previously played Caroline, Jake Ryan's girlfriend, in Hughes's first film, *Sixteen Candles*.

Principal photography for *Home Alone 3* began on December 2, 1996, shortly after the successful release of *101 Dalmatians*, and wrapped up on March 22, 1997. The movie was released on December 12, 1997, opening in third place among the four major studio films released that weekend, narrowly beating Steven Spielberg's *Amistad* but falling well behind Miramax's *Scream 2*.

For the year 1997, the film ranked sixty-sixth, far behind *Flubber*, grossing $30 million against a budget of $32 million.

Three days after filming wrapped on *Home Alone 3*, *Twister* became the first feature film released on DVD. On June 2, 1998, *Home Alone 3* was released on VHS, and on November 3, 1998, it became available on DVD. The addition of another format helped the film eventually gross around $80 million.

As expected, reviews for *Home Alone 3* were not pleasant. Variety wrote on December 7, 1997, "Five years after proving he could make box office lightning strike twice with *Home Alone 2*, this time, however, for Hughes, the law of diminishing returns catches up with him." On Siskel and Ebert's December 13, 1997, show, Gene Siskel began, "Our next film is *Home Alone 3*. Boy, has this franchise ever run out of gas." He continued, "The story makes no sense. I feel for every family that's gonna be suckered into seeing *Home Alone 3*." Roger Ebert, however, gave the film a thumbs up, which left Siskel asking, "Are you okay?"

Entertainment Weekly waited to review the film on VHS on June 5, 1998, ending their review with, "Too bad the series didn't fade out with Master Culkin's soprano" and gave it a C minus.

Although the third film didn't capture the same magic as the first two, it still made enough money to prompt discussions of another sequel in 2002, which was filmed as a pilot for a television series that never materialized. *Home Alone 4* aired as a stand-alone movie on ABC's *The Wonderful World of Disney* on November 3, 2002, without Hughes's involvement. In 2012, ABC Family Channel released *Home Alone 5: The Holiday Heist* on November 25, 2012, starring Debi Mazar, who, like Joe Pesci, had appeared in *Goodfellas* in 1990.

In 2019, Disney acquired 20th Century Fox, including the *Home Alone* franchise, and on November 12, 2021, released *Home Sweet Home Alone* on Disney+, featuring many *Saturday Night Live* alums, including Mikey Day, Kenan Thompson, and Chris Parnell. Devin Ratray, who played Buzz, Kevin's brother in the original films, reprised his role. Chris Columbus criticized the remake, stating, "Make something original, because we need more original material."

26

Reach the Rock (Finally)

A week before the release of *Flubber* and a month before *Home Alone 3*, John Hughes and Ricardo Mestres decided to dissolve Great Oaks Entertainment after producing only three films: *101 Dalmatians*, *Flubber*, and *Jack* (which starred Robin Williams as a boy who ages four times faster than normal). *Jack* had already been in development under Mestres before he and Hughes formed Great Oaks. Although all three films made money, they were critically panned, and Hughes was ready to move on.

On November 4, 1997, it was announced that Great Oaks Entertainment would be disbanded, and Ricardo Mestres would establish his own production company under Disney, named Ricardo Mestres Productions. According to *Variety*, the breakup stemmed from Hughes's "systematic" rotation of executive partners. Despite this, the split between Mestres and Hughes was amicable, as Mestres still wanted to produce films while Hughes was ready to leave Hollywood for good.

However, Hughes still had a few legal obligations in Hollywood that he couldn't avoid. Universal, his long-time nemesis, demanded that he owed them another movie. Universal had a contentious history with Hughes, having fired him from *Mr. Mom* for refusing to relocate to Hollywood, dismissing *The Breakfast Club* when it was screened, and selling *Uncle Buck* to television without informing him. In response, Hughes decided to give Universal the script that no one else wanted to direct but that he needed to complete before retiring—*Reach the Rock*.

Hughes assembled a team with minimal effort and, despite the disbanding of Great Oaks, Mestres agreed to produce the film. For this project, Hughes had his long-time assistant, William Ryan, who had worked alongside him since *Home Alone* and eventually managed Hughes Entertainment, direct the movie.

Reach the Rock is about two teenagers who make a drunken bet that one can swim out to a rock in the middle of a river—the titular "Rock." The lead character, played by Alessandro Nivola, begs his friend not to do it, and the friend ultimately drowns. Though it's not typical John Hughes fare, the film still includes some of his signature physical comedy. And the story is set in the fictional town of Shermer, Illinois, home to *Sixteen Candles*, *The Breakfast Club*, and *Ferris Bueller's Day Off*.

What makes *Reach the Rock* particularly interesting—beyond the fact that it was the last film Hughes was closely involved in outside of screenwriting—is how it rekindled his love of music and allowed him to share that passion with his son, John Hughes III. Over the years, Hughes Jr. had contributed several tracks to the soundtracks of *Dutch* and *Curly Sue*, and in 1995 Hughes Sr. helped him launch his own independent label, Hefty Records. In return, Hughes Jr. served as music supervisor on *Reach the Rock*, introducing his father to a wave of new '90s music, much as Hughes Sr. had once introduced contemporary sounds to the teens in his '80s films.

In a July 23, 1998, interview with *Chicago Reader* promoting his new label, John Hughes III mentioned that he was eager to share the soundtrack but couldn't until the movie was released. At that time, the film had been completed for over a year, but the studio didn't know what to do with it.

Universal eventually released *Reach the Rock* on October 16, 1998, but with an extremely limited release—only playing in three theaters in three cities for a one-week engagement. The film stood no chance against bigger releases like the Sandra Bullock/Nicole Kidman fantasy *Practical Magic* or even Universal's release of *Child's Play 4: Bride of Chucky*.

Surprisingly, the only critic who had supported Hughes for *Home Alone 3*, Roger Ebert, turned on him in his review of *Reach the Rock*, writing, "John Hughes, who should have donated his screenplay to a nearby day-care center for use by preschoolers in constructing paper chains." Ebert also questioned, "How can the man who made *Planes, Trains and Automobiles* have thought this material was filmable?"

It's likely Hughes had similar doubts, but he cherished working with his son on the soundtrack and listening to his son's playlist suggestions during the writing process.

Perhaps Anita Gates of *The New York Times* summed it up best in her October 16, 1998, review: "*Reach the Rock* seems like the dark side of earlier films by Mr. Hughes like *Pretty in Pink* and *Sixteen Candles*, reflecting the realization that dating the prom queen (or being her) isn't the solution to youth's problems." Hughes was trying to convey a more mature message in *Reach the Rock*, but after ten family films filled with slapstick, it was a tough sell.

27

Just Visiting and *New Port South*

As Ricardo Mestres was searching for projects under his Disney deal, he came across the French comedy film *Les Visiteurs II*. The reason this film caught Hollywood's attention in 1998 was because it was the sequel to *Les Visiteurs*, the highest-grossing film in French cinema history. *The Visitors*, as it's known in English, is a comedy about a twelfth-century knight and his squire who time travel to 1993. The original film starred Jean Reno, who had since gained recognition in American films such as *The Professional* with Natalie Portman, *The Lion King*, and the first *Mission: Impossible*.

Although a dubbed version supervised by Mel Brooks was never released, and a subtitled version distributed by Miramax in 1996 was a disappointment, Mestres believed that a remake could be a successful venture for Disney. He approached his recent ex-partner, John Hughes, to write an American version of the French screenplay, which would eventually be titled *Just Visiting*.

Given Jean Reno's newfound popularity in the U.S., he was cast in the American version alongside Christina Applegate. Hughes, as expected, set the new story in Chicago. He also collaborated with the original French screenwriters, Christian Clavier (who also appeared in the film) and Jean-Marie Poiré. However, just before filming began, Hughes withdrew from the project, reportedly unhappy with the collaboration with the original screenwriters. Hughes had not worked with another writer since *Jaws 3* and found the experience unsatisfactory.

Just Visiting began filming on April 14, 1999, and wrapped up on June 26, 1999, under the direction of Jean-Marie Gaubert, the French director of the original films. The movie was rumored to be so bad that the finished product sat on a shelf for a year. It was said that Gaubert, like Hughes, was trying to distance himself from the film. After reediting, the movie finally opened on April 6, 2001, in the U.S. and April 11, 2001, in France.

Variety magazine reported on April 4, 2001, that the budget was $50 million, but reliable sources suggested it was closer to $70 million, with some rumors pushing the final figure to $100 million, making it the most expensive film in the 100-year history of the French studio Gaumont. About twenty days later, *Variety* reported that *Just Visiting* was on the verge of bankrupting the company. The movie was a box-office disaster both in the U.S. and abroad, ending up at 169th place for the year 2001, grossing only $4 million.

Despite Hughes being mentioned in every review and industry article, no one directly blamed him for the film's failure. However, his association with the project made the likelihood of a comeback—whether as a director or producer—seem improbable. Ironically, in the same year, Hughes' protégé, Chris Columbus, directed the highest-grossing film of 2001, *Harry Potter and the Sorcerer's Stone*.

One of the few things Hughes still enjoyed was spending time with his family. In early 1999, his son James wrote a movie titled *New Port South*. John Hughes served as executive producer for the film, just as he had supported his other son, John Jr., with his music label. By November 18, 1999, the *Chicago Tribune* reported that a new Disney movie was being produced by John Hughes in and around Chicago. This meant that, once again, his friend Ricardo Mestres would help produce the film, this time under Touchstone Pictures. *New Port South* would be the final film associated with whatever was left of Hughes Entertainment.

True to form, Hughes tapped a trusted collaborator to direct the film: Kyle Cooper, the designer behind the main title sequences for *Home Alone, Curly Sue, Home Alone 2,* and *Flubber*. Although New Port South was marketed as a "teens-against-the-system" drama, it arrived quietly on September 7, 2001, in a limited test release across six markets and was ultimately treated as a straight-to-DVD title. Major outlets ignored it, but the few reviews it received singled out Cooper—long considered a virtuoso of title design—for his two-minute "mini-masterpieces."

Cooper's strengths, however, lay firmly in design and editing, not directing. As *Wired* reported in a June 1, 2004 feature, Cooper was still tinkering with the film's edit long after its release and box-office failure. He later created the iconic flip-book Marvel Studios logo that now opens every Marvel film and series, but New Port South would be his first and only feature as a director.

28

Maid in Manhattan and *Drillbit Taylor*

The 2001 film *Just Visiting* marked the last time John Hughes would be credited as a writer, and even then, it was for a script he had co-written back in 1999. Hughes might have been ready to step away from Hollywood for good, but as the famous line from *The Godfather, Part III* goes, "Just when I thought I was out, they pull me back in."

Joe Roth, who played a crucial role in Hughes's success with *Home Alone,* and Ricardo Mestres were among the few people in the industry Hughes hadn't turned his back on. On January 12, 2000, it made headlines when Roth announced he was leaving The Walt Disney Company. Roth expressed a desire to pursue more independent films, though insiders speculated his departure was due to conflicts with Michael Eisner, as several top Disney executives were leaving at the same time.

By June 7, 2000, *The New York Times* reported that Roth had secured backing for his new venture, Revolution Studios. With financial support from Sony and Fox, Revolution Studios launched with nearly $1 billion in funding. Roth's vision for Revolution was to produce films that were "inexpensive and entertaining." Unfortunately, the studio ended up making about 16 films that each cost around $70 million, and even those that grossed $90 million at the box office were considered underperformers.

Before those challenges arose, however, Roth reached out to Hughes, not only to write something new but also to coax him back into directing. Hughes handed him a script titled *The Chambermaid*. On September 18, 2000, ABC News reported that Roth's fledgling studio had *The Chambermaid* on its 2001 docket, marking Hughes's first directorial effort since 1991's *Curly Sue*.

The budget for *The Chambermaid* was set at a modest $20 million, and *Variety* reported on January 11, 2001, that Hughes would direct and produce, with Oscar-winner Hilary Swank set to star. Filming was scheduled to begin on April 1, 2001. Swank wanted Hugh Grant to be her co-star, but when he declined, she left the project in July 2001. With Swank gone and Jennifer Lopez negotiating to take on the role, Hughes began to lose enthusiasm for directing but decided to stay on as a producer.

According to *The New York Times* in November 2002, Lopez's former agent, Elaine Goldsmith-Thomas, rewrote a forty-page outline of Hughes' original screenplay, which Lopez then brought to the film. Six months later, Hughes exited the project entirely, leaving behind what was left of his script.

Hughes's original screenplay was set in the 1920s, but by October 2001, Kevin Wade (who had written 1988's *Working Girl*) was brought in to completely rewrite the script, and Hughes was relegated to a "Story by" credit. The film was retitled *Uptown Girl* and set in the present day. In July 2002, the film was still titled *Uptown Girl*, but Lopez later took credit for changing the name to *Maid in Manhattan* sometime in the fall of 2002. Once Hughes realized his script had been entirely rewritten, he requested that the studio credit the story to his pseudonym, Edmond Dantès, as he had done with *Beethoven*.

Maid in Manhattan was released on December 13, 2002, and, like most romantic comedies, received mixed reviews. However, the box office told a different story. On its opening weekend, *Maid in Manhattan* topped the charts, beating out *Star Trek X*, Disney's *The Hot Chick*, and the new James Bond and Harry Potter films (both in their fifth weeks). Worldwide, *Maid in Manhattan* grossed $155 million on a $55 million budget.

After another disheartening experience in Hollywood, this was truly the end for the genius of 1980s cinema. Hughes would never again write a movie script that saw the light of day.

As for the 2008 film *Drillbit Taylor*, it was based on a treatment Hughes had left behind at Paramount when he broke his contract after the *She's Having a Baby* debacle. After Judd Apatow's success with

The 40-Year-Old Virgin at Universal, Paramount approached Apatow with Hughes's old treatment. Apatow passed it to Seth Rogen, who turned it into a full-length feature script. Hughes had no control over the project, except to ensure the story credit again went to Edmond Dantès.

Drillbit Taylor was considered a box-office flop, grossing $49 million on a $40 million budget.

29

What Could Have Been

Regardless of his later work or the strained relationships he had with friends and colleagues, John Hughes remains a true legend and genius in the film industry. His prolific writing ability seemed limitless. Remarkably, the three films credited to his pseudonym Edmond Dantès, which were produced after he had distanced himself from them, grossed over $700 million.

After his death, it was revealed that Hughes had left behind numerous scripts, some of which he or the studios lost interest in during production, while others never made it to anyone's desk. Given that Hughes wrote *Ferris Bueller's Day Off* in just six days and *Planes, Trains and Automobiles* over a weekend, it's highly likely that there are hundreds of unrealized screenplays his estate has yet to share with the public.

Between 1983 and 1997, Paramount alone cataloged over 1,000 unproduced screenplays, including projects by other writers. Among these was a 1994 draft of *Top Gun II* (which has since been released). Another unproduced script listed in their archives is a 1982 script by Hughes titled *Motorheads vs. Sportos*. This was a modern-day *Romeo and Juliet* story set in a Chicago high school, where two star-crossed lovers find themselves caught between two feuding groups: the Motorheads and the Sportos. While the film was never made, Hughes did repurpose the terms "Motorheads" and "Sportos" in *Ferris Bueller's Day Off*, where Principal Rooney's secretary describes Ferris: "The sportos, the motorheads, geeks, sluts, bloods, wastoids, dweebies, dickheads–they all adore him. They think he's a righteous dude."

In January 1978, while *Animal House* was in pre-production, and Hughes and then editor-in-chief of National Lampoon, P. J. O'Rourke, were working on their ambitious *Sunday Newspaper Parody*, the "*Dacron, Ohio Republican-Democrat,*" for *National Lampoon* magazine, the idea of making a movie about the parody newspaper emerged. The duo began drafting a treatment that, for Hughes, quickly became almost half a screenplay titled *The History of Ohio from the Beginning of Time to the End of the Universe*. However, when they pitched the idea to the studio producing *Animal House, Animal House* had yet to be released, and the studio passed on the project. Nevertheless, Hughes and O'Rourke completed a second draft on April 14, 1980, simply titled *National Lampoon's Dacron, Ohio*. The first page of the script offers a glimpse into its premise.

> The film depicts six generations of an Ohio family. Each generation (with minor exceptions explained in the script) is represented by a Grandfather, a Father, a Mother, a Son, a Daughter, and the Son's Girl Friend. Six principal actors are called in for the film, and they play the same respective characters in each generation. In other words the actor portraying the Grandfather in the first generation will portray the Grandfather in all the succeeding generations. The actor portraying the Father in the first generation will be the Father in the succeeding generations. And so on.

The ambitious film project never got picked up, and Hughes was later approached to write the *Animal House* television series *Delta House*.

As mentioned earlier, *National Lampoon* was eager to capitalize on the success of *Animal House*. Hughes contributed to the *Delta House* TV series and then wrote *National Lampoon's Class Reunion*. Around the same time, Paramount Pictures acquired the rights to the famous 1972 illustrated sex manual by Alex Comfort, titled *The Joy of Sex*.

The book was a phenomenon, spending 11 weeks on the *New York Times* best-seller list and more than 70 weeks in the top five. Paramount, primarily interested in the title's marketability, hoped it would draw audiences to theaters. They enlisted John Hughes to write the script, which he did, creating a series of vignettes similar in style to Woody Allen's 1972 film *Everything You Always Wanted to Know About Sex (But Were Afraid to Ask)*.

According to her biography, Penny Marshall was set to direct the film, with John Belushi slated to star. However, after Belushi's untimely death, everyone involved in the project backed out. Despite this setback, Paramount, having invested heavily in the rights, decided to move forward. A year later, under the direction of Martha Coolidge, the film *The Joy of Sex* (or *National Lampoon's Joy of Sex*) was released on August 3, 1984. The movie was a box-office flop.

Rumor has it that Matty Simmons paid $250,000 to remove the *National Lampoon* name from the project, much like Hughes would later attempt to disassociate himself from certain films. Hughes had reservations about Coolidge from the start of *Some Kind of Wonderful*, eventually leading to her removal from the project. This tension may have stemmed from her directing a film he had been trying to distance himself from.

On September 5, 1983, just three months after *Mr. Mom* became a box-office success, United Press International reported that Aaron Spelling was heading to Dallas to film *Dallas Debs*. Spelling had commissioned Hughes to write a script about Dallas parents spending up to half a million dollars on extravagant debutante balls to introduce their daughters to society—a scene Spelling was familiar with as a Dallas native. Spelling described the premise as "a raucous comedy about the Dallas debutante scene, where debutante balls are graded on the size of the ice sculptures." It's unclear why the film never materialized, but it's evident that Hughes didn't appreciate working with Spelling.

Worthpoint, an online auction site, listed a first draft script by John Hughes dated June 13, 1984, titled *Fallen Angel*. Interestingly, the script contains a scene lifted directly from *Sixteen Candles*, where Anthony Michael Hall's character awkwardly dances with Molly Ringwald's character. This is peculiar since *Fallen Angel* was written just a month after the release of *Sixteen Candles*. It's possible that Hughes didn't anticipate *Sixteen Candles* becoming a hit or a cult classic. In *Fallen Angel*, the character Marissa performs a solo *Flashdance* imitation, unaware she's being watched, and is told, "Very hot, babe. Very hot." This mirrors the scene where Hall's character says the same line while dancing with Ringwald in *Sixteen Candles*.

On February 10, 2010, *Vanity Fair* published an article by David Kamp featuring interviews with Anthony Michael Hall and Molly Ringwald. Both actors revealed that while filming *The Breakfast Club*, John Hughes had shared with them ideas for future "musical" projects he envisioned them starring in. Hall's project was tentatively titled *The Last Good Year*, a humorous take on 1962 as the "last good year" in music before the British Invasion led by The Beatles. For Ringwald, Hughes began writing a script called *Lovecats*, inspired by The Cure's song "The Lovecats," which she had shared with him. Although these projects never materialized, Hughes created mix tapes for each actor, showcasing the soundtracks he imagined for the films. It was also during this time that Ringwald introduced Hughes to the Psychedelic Furs' song "Pretty in Pink," which later inspired the movie of the same name.

On February 10, 1991, Joe Roth announced 20th Century Fox's lineup of films for that year during a lunch event. With *Home Alone* breaking box office records, Roth revealed three new John Hughes projects alongside *Dutch*, which had already been completed. The films announced were *The Nanny*, *The Bugster*, and *Ball 'n' Chain*. However, after the underwhelming performance of *Dutch* and *Curly Sue* (which was produced by Warner Brothers), these projects were reportedly reevaluated.

In the early 1990s, the story of Huck Finn was a hot property in Hollywood, with three competing versions in development by Fox, Tristar, and Disney. Fox had commissioned Hughes to create their version, titled *Black Cat Bone: The Return of Huckleberry Finn*. The script was completed, and in November 1991, the *Pittsburgh Press* reported that Hughes was set to begin filming *Home Alone 2* on December 9, 1991, with principal photography for *Black Cat Bone* scheduled to start on March 16, 1992. Hughes Entertainment and 20th Century Fox even produced a promotional poster for the film, featuring a yellow moon over a city skyline (possibly Chicago) with the title in bold black letters. However, after Disney released their own adaptation, *The Adventures of Huck Finn*, on April 2, 1993, which performed poorly at the box office, all other Huck Finn projects, including Hughes's, were halted.

Before the release of *Home Alone 2*, Hughes was poised to shift genres once again, this time into movie musicals. Warner Brothers had plans for him to create big-screen remakes of *The Pajama Game* and *Damn Yankees*, two musicals originally produced by the studio in 1957 and 1958, respectively. On October 6, 1992, it was announced that Warner Brothers had reacquired the rights to *The Pajama Game* for Hughes to write, produce, and possibly direct. Additionally, according to author Kirk Honeycutt, Hughes had completed a script for *Damn Yankees*. Unfortunately, neither project ever came to fruition.

In 1993, as *Home Alone 2* continued its strong box office performance and Hughes was in the middle of producing *Baby's Day*

Out, Warner Brothers approached him to rewrite *Good Dog, Carl*, based on a series of children's books by Alexandra Day. The studio had previously enlisted David Simkins, the writer of *Adventures in Babysitting*, to adapt the story, but they were dissatisfied with the result.

On March 23, 1993, *Variety* reported that Hughes was brought on to write, produce, and direct the film, which was about a toddler who is kidnapped and then rescued by a Rottweiler named Carl. Warner Brothers was so eager to have Hughes on board that they fired the previous director, David Mickey Evans. However, after *Baby's Day Out* underperformed at the box office, with critics pointing out its similarities to the *Good Dog, Carl* series, the project was ultimately canceled.

On July 26, 1996, Hughes finished a script titled *Tickets*. The story revolves around a group of teenage strangers who camp out overnight in freezing temperatures, all in pursuit of tickets to their favorite band's farewell concert. *Tickets* shares similarities with *The Breakfast Club*, as it primarily focuses on the interactions and conversations between four or five main characters as they wait in line throughout the night. Here's an excerpt from the script:

```
EXT. CLUB

Asa and Leslie are sitting on the camp mattress,
in front of the grill, now glowing hot with
construction trims. Tom is sleeping. The portable
PLAYS MUSIC SOFTLY.

                    LESLIE

I hate four o'clock in the morning.

                     ASA

I don't have a watch. I was worried it might
get stolen off me so I didn't bring it.

                    LESLIE

I don't need a watch to know what time it
is. This feels like four.

                     ASA
               (genuinely inquisitive)

How does four feel?

                    LESLIE

Lonely.
```

                        ASA
                  (after a pause)

How old are you, really?

                       LESLIE

Fifteen. I was born New Year's Day 1982.

                        ASA

I was born in May.

                       LESLIE
                  (with a sad smile)

Rough winds do shake the darling buds
of May, and summer's lease hath all too
short a date. That's from a poem. At my
grandmother's house in the bedroom I used
to sleep in, it was part of the wallpaper,
along the top. I still remember it. I
probably always will. Do me a big favor.
Don't feel sorry for me. I don't need
anything and I don't want anything. My life
doesn't suck.

                        ASA

I didn't say it did.

                       LESLIE

Twenty years from now, I might be up in your
neighborhood, married to some guy, have kids
and a house, and look like I went to college
and you could meet me and not ever know that
I was me.

Tickets never made it to production, as any potential progress was halted when New Line Cinema released *Detroit Rock City* in August 1999. The film, which had a similar premise centered around fans of the band Kiss, was a box-office failure, effectively shutting down any further interest in *Tickets*.

30

The Ones That Almost Made It

Oil and Vinegar

On July 3, 1988, the *Los Angeles Times* reported that John Hughes was set to return to Universal to direct a new script in the fall, titled *Oil and Vinegar*. The film was slated to star Matthew Broderick and Molly Ringwald. Broderick was to play a traveling salesman driving across the country on the way to his wedding. Along the way, he picks up Ringwald's character, a hitchhiker, and they end up stranded in a remote motel room, engaging in an all-night conversation about the complexities of coming of age as adults.

Those who had read the script remarked on its strong resemblance to *The Breakfast Club*. Hughes had given the script to Broderick, who expressed his fascination, noting that it was an even more intimate experiment than *The Breakfast Club*. Ringwald, however, mentioned that the script needed some rewrites, which Hughes reportedly refused to do.

The script had been written about two years prior, and Hughes had initially approached director Alan Metter to gauge his interest in directing *Oil and Vinegar*. Metter, who shared an agent with Hughes, was coming off the success of Rodney Dangerfield's *Back to School*, a surprise hit in 1986 that outperformed *Ferris Bueller's Day Off* at the box office.

Metter theorized that Hughes typically worked on two projects a year—one he directed himself and another he produced but didn't direct, which he referred to as Hughes' annual "B" film. Despite his appreciation for the script, Metter chose not to take a back seat to Hughes, whom he had bested at the box office that year. In a 2009 interview with *Filmmaker* magazine, Metter admitted that turning down *Oil and Vinegar* was the biggest mistake of his life, as he was never offered a script that good again.

Howard Deutch, another director who read the script, was equally impressed. According to Jon Cryer's memoir, Deutch told Cryer that *Oil and Vinegar* was the best script Hughes had ever written. However, in an August 18, 2014, interview with *New York Magazine*, Deutch revealed that his then girlfriend, Lea Thompson, advised him against taking on the project, warning that he would be overwhelmed by filming and preparing two movies simultaneously, as he was already directing *Some Kind of Wonderful*. Deutch's hesitation apparently offended Hughes, who viewed the reluctance as a betrayal. This ultimately led to Deutch being fired from *Some Kind of Wonderful and* his office door reportedly padlocked.

Oil and Vinegar had the potential to be a remarkable transitional piece for Hughes, bridging his teen-focused films with more adult themes. However, the project never moved forward. Fortunately for Hughes, the following year saw the release of *Planes, Trains and Automobiles*, which was met with critical and commercial success, easing his transition into more mature storytelling without the need for *Oil and Vinegar*.

Bartholomew vs. Neff

While John Hughes was redefining his career with the adult comedy smash *Planes, Trains and Automobiles*, Arnold Schwarzenegger was also surprising audiences by transitioning into comedy with *Twins*. Starring alongside Danny DeVito, Schwarzenegger turned *Twins* into a sleeper hit, grossing over $216 million on an $18-million budget. He then followed up seamlessly with blockbuster successes in *Terminator 2* and *Total Recall*, which together grossed nearly a billion dollars. Schwarzenegger's comedic streak continued with *Kindergarten Cop*, which added another $100 million to his box office tally.

In contrast, Sylvester Stallone, who was often seen as Schwarzenegger's rival, struggled at the box office with a series of late '80s flops, including *Cobra, Over the Top, Lock Up*, and *Rocky V*. Seeing Schwarzenegger's successful foray into comedy, Stallone decided to try his hand at the genre.

On July 30, 1990, the *Los Angeles Times* reported that Stallone and John Candy were set to star in a John Hughes-written and directed film titled *Bartholomew vs. Neff*, a comedy about feuding neighbors. The film was slated to begin production in the summer of 1991, with shooting planned in the Chicago suburbs. Stallone was cast as a former professional baseball player, while Candy would play a corporate banker.

Two days later, on August 1, 1990, the Cincinnati Enquirer ran a headline that read, "Yo, Stallone, you look pretty in pink," highlighting the unexpected pairing of Stallone with Hughes. Stallone expressed his enthusiasm for the project, stating, "I am very excited about working with a director with the stature of John Hughes. I have long been a fan of his films, which capture the truly comic side of everyday life."

Carolco Pictures—the studio behind *Terminator 2* and *Rambo*—was enthusiastic about producing *Bartholomew vs. Neff* and even began promoting the film before it entered production, going so far as to put up a billboard announcing the project. But momentum stalled when *Home Alone* became an unexpected phenomenon, ultimately the highest-grossing comedy of all time. Hughes then shifted his attention to writing the sequel and directing *Curly Sue*, pushing *Bartholomew vs. Neff* to the sidelines.

A series of setbacks pushed the project even further out of reach. *Curly Sue* underperformed at the box office; Hughes's relationship with John Candy deteriorated after Candy turned down roles in *Dutch*, *Dennis the Menace*, and *Home Alone 2*; and Sylvester Stallone's attempts at comedy—*Oscar* and *Stop! Or My Mom Will Shoot*—were met with critical and commercial failure.

Despite these complications, Carolco remained interested. Stallone and Candy were still working with the studio on other films, keeping the project technically alive. But Candy's sudden death during the making of *Wagons East* and Stallone's pivot back to action with *Cliffhanger* sealed its fate, and *Bartholomew vs. Neff* was quietly abandoned for good.

Peanuts

In November 1992, while Hughes was working on *Dennis the Menace* and collaborating with comic-strip creator Hank Ketcham, he began considering an even more ambitious project: a live-action movie adaptation of Charles Schulz's iconic *Peanuts* characters, including Charlie Brown and Lucy.

In 1967, Charles Schulz granted the rights to an off-Broadway musical titled *You're a Good Man, Charlie Brown*. The musical was highly successful, running for over three years. However, when it transitioned to Broadway, it did not perform as well, which made Schulz hesitant to pursue a live-action movie adaptation.

Hughes personally traveled to Schulz's home in Santa Rosa, California, to discuss the potential project. Despite Schulz's well-known reluctance to let others into his *Peanuts* world, he and Hughes hit it off. Schulz was impressed by Hughes's respect for his work and his commitment to carefully reviewing forty-two years of daily strips before attempting a screenplay. Hughes assured Schulz that he would approach the script like an editor, staying true to the essence of the beloved comic strip.

On November 15, 1992, *Variety* reported that Warner Brothers had acquired the movie rights to *Peanuts* and had commissioned John Hughes to write and produce the film, with the clear understanding that he would not direct it. The plan was for Hughes to begin working on the script in December and deliver it to the studio by the spring of 1993. Since Hughes had a non-exclusive seven-picture deal with 20th Century Fox, his involvement with Warner Brothers on this project posed no contractual issues.

However, when *Dennis the Menace* was released in June 1993, it received overwhelmingly negative reviews. Despite its commercial success, the film did not achieve the blockbuster status of *Home Alone*, which had become the new standard for Hughes's movies. The lukewarm reception of *Dennis the Menace* led to a halt in Hughes's plans to adapt *Peanuts* into a live-action film.

The Bee

In 1989, Hughes had grand plans not only to continue his prolific output of writing, producing, and directing but also to reforest the land he had purchased, known as Redwing Farms, in Western Illinois. He conducted extensive research, much like he would later do for projects like *Peanuts*, into the botanical and dendrological history of the property, aiming to restore it to its pre-cultivation state.

During this time, Hughes worked with a team of landscapers and farmers, growing crops and raising cattle. As was typical for Hughes, this hands-on project sparked an idea for a screenplay—a film about an architect who, while trying to complete a project, becomes distracted by a bee. The entire movie would revolve around the bee causing the architect to inadvertently destroy his own house and, metaphorically, his life.

Following the success of *Home Alone*, Hughes was more prominent in Hollywood than ever before—a remarkable feat considering his previous successes with *The Breakfast Club, Ferris Bueller's Day Off*, and *Planes, Trains and Automobiles*. *Home Alone* catapulted Hughes to a new level of fame and influence, allowing him to demand budgets typically reserved for directors like James Cameron or Steven Spielberg. Hughes envisioned *The Bee* as his next big-budget passion project. His deal with Fox allowed him to greenlight any project with a budget of $15 million or less, but after *Home Alone*, he requested a $50 million budget for *The Bee*.

In the early 1990s, $50 million was a substantial sum, usually allocated to action blockbusters like *Terminator 2, Total Recall*, or *Die Hard 2*. Even *Back to the Future Part III* was limited to a budget of only $40 million. The challenge with *The Bee* was that it required advanced special effects, which were still in their early stages. Hughes was so enthusiastic about the project that he hired Industrial Light and Magic to begin work on a mechanical bee.

While juggling multiple projects in 1991, including the sequel to *Home Alone*, Hughes spent considerable time with Daniel Stern during the filming of *Home Alone 2*. In an interview with *Entertainment Weekly* after Hughes' death, Stern revealed that he and Hughes became great friends, bonding over their shared sense of humor. They laughed together on set, and as their friendship grew, Stern expressed his interest in directing. Hughes, recognizing Stern's potential, showed him the script for *The Bee* and invited him to direct the film. Stern, who had directed several episodes of *The Wonder Years*, was thrilled and began working with Hughes on the script.

Hughes even invited Stern and his family to Redwing Farm, much like he had done with John Candy, to strengthen their bond. Although the script for *The Bee* reportedly contained only about ten pages of dialogue, Hughes and Stern were hopeful that Steve Martin would star in the film.

However, when Joe Roth left Fox for Disney in early 1993, 20th Century Fox became hesitant to fund *The Bee* at the $50 million budget Hughes requested. Roth did leave Stern another project to direct, *Rookie of the Year*, which was a moderate success. On June 15, 1993, *Variety* announced that Hughes had taken *The Bee* to Warner Brothers, with plans to begin shooting in January 1994 in and around Chicago.

By August 1993, *The Chicago Tribune* reported that Hughes and his crew were scouting locations for the film, describing it as a story about an out-of-town developer who clashes with a rural community, led by a beekeeper, determined to protect their land.

Despite these efforts, Hughes began to lose interest in the project by late 1993, and in May 1994, Warner Brothers placed *The Bee* in turnaround, just as they had previously done with *Home Alone*. On June 24, 1994, Hughes signed a deal with Joe Roth at Disney, initially intended to produce *The Bee*. However, with the failure of the movie *Baby's Day Out* on July 1, 1994, with its $50 million in special effects, *The Bee* was shelved, and Hughes's enthusiasm for Hollywood began to wane.

Interestingly, in 2022, Netflix released a television series called *Man vs. Bee* starring Rowan Atkinson. The premise involves a housesitter engaged in a battle with a bumblebee inside an elegant mansion. Rumors suggest that Atkinson was shown the script for Hughes's *The Bee* while Hughes was in London meeting with British talent. However, Hughes's name is not credited anywhere in the Netflix show.

The Grigsbys Go Broke

After Hughes's death, his family revealed numerous scripts that were either unfinished or never produced. Among these was a completed second draft of a script dated March 4, 2003, titled *The Grigsbys Go Broke*. This script was brought to the attention of Paramount. *The Grigsbys Go Broke* centers around a wealthy Chicago family who lose their fortune and are forced to move to a less affluent neighborhood.

In March 2010, following an Oscar tribute to John Hughes that reignited interest in his work, *The Hollywood Reporter* mentioned on March 7, 2010, that there were rumors Paramount was considering picking up *The Grigsbys Go Broke* for production, with family friend Joe Roth set to produce. The trade magazine noted the disappointing outcome of Hughes's last film, *Drillbit Taylor*, but emphasized that Paramount would "jump at the chance to take part in another Hughes creation." Despite the buzz, the project stalled for several years.

On February 6, 2013, *Deadline* reported that Paramount was reviving the project, with Jim Hecht, known for his success with the animated film *Ice Age: The Meltdown*, hired to rewrite Hughes's original 2003 script. Although the film has yet to be made, the script retains the essence of a classic Hughes comedy.

In *The Grigsbys Go Broke*, as the Grigsby family adjusts to their new "lower-class" neighborhood, they receive help from a welcoming committee of neighbors, including a kind elderly woman named Mrs. Gummer. Gracie Grigsby, the four-year-old daughter, struggles to cope with the family's new reality and has recently been expelled from "Lil Stinkers Day Care." The interactions between Gracie and Mrs. Gummer capture the same charm and humor reminiscent of the dynamic between Macaulay Culkin and John Candy in *Uncle Buck*:

```
Mrs. Gummer is making lemonade. Gracie peeks into the
room from the screen porch. Mrs. Gummer looks over
her shoulder and smiles.

                    MRS. GUMMER

          Are you going to help serve
          refreshments?

                    GRACIE

          Do I look like a waitress?

                    MRS. GUMMER

          I'm Mrs. Gummer. Are you Gracie?

                    GRACIE

          Who told you?

                    MRS. GUMMER

          Your sister.

                    GRACIE

          She has a big mouth.

Harold pokes his head in.

                    HAROLD

          All set.

                    MRS. GUMMER

          Thank you. (to Gracie) That's Mr.
          Chamberlain. He's your next-door
          neighbor.

                    GRACIE

          He's fat.

                    MRS. GUMMER

          I'm a little fat myself
```

                    GRACIE

At least you're honest.

                    MRS. GUMMER

I'll bet you a nickel that one day you
and I are going to friends.

                    GRACIE

You won't live that long.

                    MRS. GUMMER

Oh, I think I might. I have a lot
of little friends. The moms in the
neighborhood who work leave their
children with me during the day.

                    GRACIE

Do you have a care provider's license?

                    MRS. GUMMER
                  (chuckles)

I have something much, much better. I
have the trust of my neighbors.

                    GRACIE

Good luck in court.

                    MRS. GUMMER

Maybe when your folks go to work on
Monday, you'll come visit me.

                    GRACIE

I'd rather eat kitty litter.

Mrs. Gummer gives Gracie a smile and returns to the
kitchen.

INT. KITCHEN

Mrs. Gummer continues making her lemonade at the
kitchen sink. Gracie peeks into the kitchen and
watches her from behind. Mrs. Gummer senses the
little eyes on her. She grins.

                    MRS. GUMMER
                (without turning around)
                I'm famous for my lemonade.

31

The Death of John Hughes

In the latter half of the 2000s, John Hughes continued to write prolifically. His son James noted that while Hughes was a latecomer to email, once he embraced it, he composed what David Kamp described in a 2010 *Vanity Fair* article as "thought avalanches":

> These emails were lavish, interdisciplinary discourses that touched on everything from current events and political scandals to the Chicago Blackhawks, classic films he'd watched on TCM, authors featured on C-SPAN's *Booknotes*, the trees he was planting, and the obscure hillbilly music he was compiling—whatever happened to be on his mind.

During this time, Hughes and Vince Vaughn would talk all night, and as Vaughn recalls, "We'd be literally engaged in conversation for 12 hours about anything, but especially music. His knowledge of music was incredible."

James Hughes reflected on his father's later years, saying, "In his later years, it was sort of his primary job to ingest all this material and riff on it." Hughes was known for writing long, passionate emails to friends and correspondents, and he frequently exchanged letters with fans. One such fan, a teenager at the time, shared some of his letters online after his death. In one, Hughes wrote: "You've already received more letters from me than any living relative of mine has received to date. Truly, hope all is well with you and high school isn't as painful as I portray it. Believe in yourself. Think about the future once a day and keep doing what you're doing."

On May 24, 2009, Hughes was spotted at the United Center in Chicago, attending a game where the Detroit Red Wings faced the Chicago Blackhawks in the Stanley Cup Western Conference Final.

That summer, Hughes's son James was living in New York City and had just welcomed a son. On August 5, 2009, John Hughes and his wife flew to New York City to visit their new grandson. The next day, while taking a walk near his hotel, a place he had frequented in his youth, Hughes suffered a heart attack. Despite having quit smoking in 2001, the years of chain-smoking had taken their toll.

Hughes left behind a legacy of groundbreaking films and numerous unfinished or unpublished scripts. He also left over 300 small red Moleskine pocket notebooks. Hughes never went anywhere without one, using them to jot down ideas as they came to him. These notebooks are filled with drawings and caricatures, and the last one he had with him when he died contained a detailed sketch of the hotel room he was staying in while in New York City.

On August 11, 2009, Molly Ringwald wrote an Op-Ed piece in *The New York Times* expressing her sorrow over losing contact with John Hughes after the making of *Pretty in Pink*. She likened Hughes to Peter Pan, noting how deeply he would be hurt when the Darling children chose to leave Neverland, warning them that they could never return. Hughes had a tendency to cut people out of his life in a manner akin to a child, but after his death, he was remembered with great affection by those who knew him.

In March 2010, during the Oscars, several of Hughes' most iconic actors, including Matthew Broderick, Jon Cryer, Macaulay Culkin, Anthony Michael Hall, Judd Nelson, Molly Ringwald, and Ally Sheedy, paid tribute to him. Matthew Broderick acknowledged Hughes's family—his wife Nancy, his sons John Hughes III and James, and their wives—who all stood up and took a bow in honor of their late patriarch.

In 2020, during the COVID-19 pandemic, Josh Gad created a web series titled *Reunited Apart*, which featured virtual reunions of casts and crews from legendary films. The sixth episode, aired on June 29, 2020, focused on *Ferris Bueller's Day Off*. Matthew Broderick, Alan Ruck, Mia Sara, Jennifer Grey, and Ben Stein came together to share their experiences making the film, each speaking from their respective homes via Zoom. The episode concluded with a tribute to John Hughes, set to the Simple Minds' "Don't You (Forget About Me)." The montage featured old photos of Hughes with the casts of his films, interspersed with scenes from those movies where the actors still alive in 2020, and in lockdown, recited their iconic lines over their phones. These were blended with clips from Hughes interviews, where he discussed his creative process and his hopes for what audiences would take away from his films.

The legendary quotes from John Hughes' array of personalities during his lifetime included:

Molly Ringwald (52) from *Sixteen Candles*: "They fucking forgot my birthday."

Anthony Michael Hall (52) from *The Breakfast Club*: "Chicks cannot hold their smoke. That's what it is."

Chevy Chase (77) and his meltdown from *Vacation*: ". . .we're gonna have so much fucking fun we're going to need plastic surgery to remove the goddamn smiles."

Ilan Mitchell-Smith (51) from *Weird Science*: "Why are we wearing bras on our heads?"

Steve Martin (75) from *Planes, Trains and Automobiles*: "Those aren't pillows!!!"

Jon Cryer (55) from *Pretty in Pink*: "Drinking and driving don't mix. That's why I ride a bike."

Julia Louis-Dreyfus (59) from *Christmas Vacation*, "If you want to come in, you're going to have to breakdown the goddamn door."

Alisan Porter (39) from *Curly Sue*: "All you learn from the art museum is how to keep your mouth shut and how to walk without making squeaky sounds with your shoes."

Judd Nelson (61) from *The Breakfast Club*: "Screws fall out all the time, the world is an imperfect place."

Jane Krakowski (52) from *Vacation*: "I'm going steady and I French kiss ... yeah but Daddy says I'm the best."

Andrew McCarthy (58) from *Pretty in Pink*: "I believed in you, I just didn't believe in me. I love you. Always."

Laurie Metcalf (65) from *Uncle Buck*: "My name is Marcie Dahlgren-Frost. Dahlgren is my maiden name, Frost is my married name. I'm single again, but I never bothered to remove the Frost. And I get compliments on the hyphen."

Michael Keaton (69) from *Mr. Mom*: "You gave me some real good advice once, so let me give you some of my own, it's real easy to forget what's important, so don't."

The tribute concludes with a montage of scenes from Hughes's films as "Don't You (Forget About Me)" plays, leading to Judd Nelson's iconic fist-in-the-air moment from *The Breakfast Club* and a title card reading, "John Hughes 1950–2009." The scene then cuts to 66-year-old Catherine O'Hara at the airport in *Home Alone 2* humorously screaming, "Kevin!" Finally, the montage shifts to a young Matthew Broderick in *Ferris Bueller's Day Off*, delivering his famous line, "I said it before, and I'll say it again: life moves pretty fast. If you don't stop and look around once in a while, you could miss it." The tribute ends with 76-year-old Ben Stein saying, "God Bless America, God Bless Ferris."

For these celebrities to come together eleven years after John Hughes' passing, nearly forty years after those films were made, and enthusiastically repeat such iconic lines speaks volumes about Hughes' impact. His short yet influential journey left an indelible mark on countless people and generations.

Author's Notes

Like many others, I've been a devoted John Hughes fan for years. I vividly remember seeing *The Breakfast Club* in theaters when it first came out, and I was blown away by its uniqueness. I wasn't even sure if I liked it at first, but I was undeniably fascinated by it. I loved *Pretty in Pink* the first time I saw it, and *Planes, Trains and Automobiles* was an instant classic for me from the moment it was released.

As I began writing this book, I realized just how extensive and varied Hughes's work truly was. I knew about *Home Alone* but hadn't fully appreciated his later work on films like *101 Dalmatians*, *Miracle on 34th Street*, or even *Baby's Day Out*. Diving into Hughes' complete body of work was utterly fascinating.

As a professor at Montclair State University in New Jersey, where I teach a course on 80s films, John Hughes naturally became a central topic. Comparing Hughes's comedies to those of Harold Ramis in the 1980s, especially considering their collaboration and the similarities in their careers, provided a whirlwind of information. Both Hughes and Ramis emerged from the *National Lampoon* scene, and both passed away far too young, possibly due to their shared habit of smoking. After working together on *Vacation*, the two took different paths in defining 1980s comedy, but there's no doubt they were instrumental in shaping that era in cinema.

Interestingly, none of Hughes's unproduced scripts have been produced posthumously. It seems that, even in the ruthless world of Hollywood, where people who grew up on Hughes' films now hold power, there's a reverence for his legacy that keeps them from tampering with it.

It's difficult to explain why someone with the visionary talent behind *The Breakfast Club* shifted towards more slapstick comedies later in his career. After researching this book, one could argue that perhaps he did it on purpose, to challenge our expectations. But I don't believe for a minute that Hughes ever stopped caring about his projects, right up until the day he died. Even with *Maid in Manhattan* in 2002, he was embarrassed that his name was associated with the film after it was rewritten.

People often ask how Hughes was able to write teens so authentically, and the answer, after writing this book, seems simple: as Molly Ringwald said in her 2009 Op-Ed for *The New York Times*, Hughes was like Peter Pan. He never truly grew up. He took everything personally, and unfortunately, Hollywood is not a business for those who do. It's fascinating to see how he distanced himself from people when he found out they were thinking of working with other directors; getting upset at John Candy for partying too late the day before a shoot on the set of *Uncle Buck*. Perhaps he was angry he wasn't included and then tried to find a new friend in Ed O'Neill or Daniel Stern because he was upset with Candy.

On the flip side, it was an actor's dream to have someone like John Hughes love them as much as he did, which translated to his working with the same actors repeatedly. I believe Hughes felt he could keep all of them employed all the time. For instance, if someone like John Candy needed to make money, Hughes would just write them a movie. However, actors are also artists who need to explore new opportunities. Hughes became upset when Candy wanted to work with Oliver Stone on *JFK* or when Anthony Michael Hall wanted to work with Stanley Kubrick.

I'm not sure if Hughes ever fully understood his own status in the world. That's often the issue with comedy; as funny as it may be, it's rarely taken seriously. Sure, *Home Alone* made half a billion dollars, but why wasn't it nominated for any major awards that year (besides John Williams for the score)? Hughes chose a genre that didn't provide the accolades he seemed to crave, the validation he needed.

However, his fellow actors and directors deeply appreciated his talent, even if Hughes didn't always recognize it. As I mentioned earlier, Hughes created his own film genre within his lifetime, and that's an incredibly rare achievement. Everyone wanted to be in a John Hughes movie, but they also wanted to work with other greats like Steven Spielberg, and that didn't always sit well with Hughes.

The fact is, John Hughes left us with a legacy of greatness. His films not only stand the test of time but continue to grow in esteem, much like *The Wizard of Oz*. Every teenager still resonates with *The Breakfast Club*—an almost impossible feat. It's easy to see why a family film like *Home Alone* or *The Wizard of Oz* would endure, but *The Breakfast Club* is a miracle of existence. And *Ferris Bueller's Day Off*, who wouldn't appreciate the fantasy of being the most popular kid in school like Ferris? Add *Sixteen Candles*, which remains a funny, entertaining movie with an incredible cast, along with *Planes, Trains and Automobiles*, and you have five films that any up-and-coming director would kill to have on their resume.

These aren't just comedy classics; they are films that rival the likes of *The Godfather* or *Some Like It Hot*. I believe Hughes's intense lifestyle—juggling multiple projects, staying up all night blasting music with coffee and cigarettes, always writing the next big thing, and stressing over relationships—ultimately contributed to his early demise. But what a legacy he left behind.

Bibliography

Alexander, B., "'Pretty In Pink' still shocks at 35 with changed ending: Andie chose rich Blane over poor Duckie," *USA Today*, February 26, 2021

Alexander, B., "Steve Martin has no regrets about 19 f-bombs in 'Planes, Trains and Automobiles' car rental tirade," *USA Today*, November 24, 2022

Alter, E., "Jennifer Connelly's provocative poster and other 'Career Opportunities' secrets on the movie's 30th anniversary," *Yahoo Entertainment*, March 29, 2021

Bailey, J., "'Planes, Trains and Automobiles' at 35: An Oral History of One of the Most Beloved Road Movies Ever Made," *Vanity Fair*, November 22, 2022

Bierly, M., "Reminiscing with Jon Cryer about 'Pretty in Pink,'" *Entertainment Weekly*, August 24, 2006

Borrelli, C., "'The Breakfast Club' 30 years later: Don't you forget about them," *Chicago Tribune*, February 17, 2015

Botes, Z, "35 Trivia Tidbits About 'The Great Outdoors' on Its 35th Anniversary," Cracked.com, June 17, 2023

Brew, S., "The Bee: The $50 Million John Hughes Movie That Fell Apart," Den of Geek.com, April 9, 2018

Brown, J., "Sitting Down with 'Mystic Pizza' Screenwriter Amy Jones," The Script Lab, June 12, 2015

Burch, J., "Casting *Sixteen Candles*," Arrow Video, 2020

Carter, B., "Him Alone," *The New York Times*, August 4, 1991

Crow, D., "Planes, Trains and Automobiles: How Tricking Steve Martin Changed the Ending," Den of Geek.com, November 22, 2023

Evans, B., "The Lost Projects of John Hughes," Vulture.com, July 12, 2012

Fechner, J., "'Home Alone 2: Lost in Milwaukee': The holiday classic that never was," *Spectrum News 1*, December 18, 2023

Fields, A. B., Correspondence with John Hughes, We'll Know When We Get There.com, August 6, 2009

Fleming, C., "Roth lands at Disney in all-stops-out deal," *Variety*, November 2, 1992

Gora, S., *You Couldn't Ignore Me If You Tried: The Brat Pack, John Hughes, and Their Impact on a Generation* (Penguin/Random House, 2011)

Greiving, T., "'Some Kind of Wonderful' Is the Only John Hughes Movie That Fully Embraced L.A.," *Los Angeles Magazine*, March 5, 2021

Guerrasio, J., "John Candy was paid just $414 for his cameo in 'Home Alone'—and the film's director said he always felt bitter about it," *Business Insider*, December 24, 2023

Haanen, R., Jeremiah Chechik Interview, November 2021

Haddon, C., "It's Time to Recognize 'Mr. Mom' As a Feminist Classic," Substack, November 28, 2023

Ham, W., "Straight Outta Sherman: An Interview with John Hughes," *Lollipop Magazine*, April 1, 1999

Harrington, N., Television Academy Foundation Ed O'Neill Interview, April 3, 2013

Hemphill, J., "'Am I Going to Have to Reshoot Half of This Movie? Howard Deutch on "Some Kind of Wonderful," *Filmmaker Magazine*, February 18, 2021

Hirsch, P., *A Long Time Ago in a Cutting Room Far, Far Away: My Fifty Years Editing Hollywood Hits—Star Wars, Carrie, Ferris Bueller's Day Off, Mission: Impossible, and More* (Chicago Review Press, 2019)

Honeycutt, K., "How the Female Stars of 'The Breakfast Club' Fought to Remove a Sexist Scene, and Won," *Vanity Fair*, March 12, 2015

Honeycutt, K., *John Hughes: A Life in Film: The Genius Behind Ferris Bueller, The Breakfast Club, Home Alone, and More* (Racepoint Publishing, 2015)

Ibrahim, S., "Anthony Michael Hall regrets passing on 'Ferris Bueller' and 'Pretty in Pink,'" *New York Post*, October 8, 2021

Kaldey, L., "(NOT) YOUR SONG," *Los Angeles Times*, October 25, 1987

Kamp, D., "Sweet Bard of Youth," *Vanity Fair*, February 10, 2010

Kehr, D., "FILM IN REVIEW; 'Just Visiting,'" *The New York Times*, April 6, 2001

Knelman, M., *John Candy; The Life of: Laughing on the Outside* (Viking Press, 1996)

Krol, C., "Psychedelic Furs frontman says 'Pretty In Pink' filmmaker John Hughes misinterpreted song," *New Musical Express Magazine*, August 17, 2020

Leddone, R., "The Untold Story of 'National Lampoon's Christmas Vacation,'" *Rolling Stone*, December 11, 2020

Lenker, M. L., "'John Hughes was a romantic. He was in love with love': An oral history of Some Kind of Wonderful," *Entertainment Weekly*, February 11, 2019

Libbey, D., "Cool Runnings Star Says He's Never Forgotten A Comment John Candy Made On Set Before His Death," Cinemablend.com, October 6, 2023

Lyman, R., "The Long Search for a Perfect Geek," *Knight-Ridder Newspapers,* May 21, 1984

Mann, Sophie, "A Christmas miracle! 'Home Alone' almost NEVER got made due to Warner Bros. pulling funding—and the iconic Marv character was almost played by Dan Roebuck," *Daily Mail*, December 25, 2023

Murphy, E., "12 'Ferris Bueller' Fun Facts (From the Family That Actually Lived There)," ABC News, November 8, 2013

Plume, K., "Rise and Fall (and Rise) of a Hollywood Director: An Interview with Patrick Read Johnson," IGN, March 4, 2001

Ramis H., "John Hughes Remembered: Harold Ramis (director of 'Vacation')," Dotdash Meredith, August 13, 2009

Sage, T., "Why Two Hours Was Cut From 'Planes, Trains and Automobiles,'" Ultimate Classic Rock.com, November 25, 2021

Sturges, F., "Don't You (Forget About Me)—Simple Minds have had a fraught relationship with their biggest hit," *Financial Times*, September 2, 2019

Thompson, S., "Inside 80s Classic 'Pretty In Pink' With Director Howard Deutch," *Forbes*, June 17, 2020

Vorel, J., "Explore the Lost, 3-Hour Original Cut of *Uncle Buck*, With Unearthed John Candy Footage," *Paste Magazine*, January 7, 2021

Waxman, O., "Molly Ringwald Talks About the Most Embarrassing Part of Filming 'The Breakfast Club,'" *Time*, February 15, 2015

Wilkenson, A., "*Home Alone 2* and the Wild, Weird Origin Story of the Talkboy," *Vanity Fair*, November 18, 2022

Zaleski, A., "Why the 'Pretty in Pink' Soundtrack Still Matters," Ultimate Classic Rock.com, March 2, 2021